C000093952

Turning Pain into Purpose

Chronicles for the Brokenhearted

LORETTA EVERSON

ISBN 979-8-88685-390-2 (paperback)
ISBN 979-8-88685-391-9 (digital)

Copyright © 2022 by Loretta Everson

All rights reserved. No part of this publication may be reproduced, distributed, or transmitted in any form or by any means, including photocopying, recording, or other electronic or mechanical methods without the prior written permission of the publisher. For permission requests, solicit the publisher via the address below.

Christian Faith Publishing
832 Park Avenue
Meadville, PA 16335
www.christianfaithpublishing.com

Printed in the United States of America

I dedicate this book first and foremost to my heavenly Father, who did not give me a spirit of fear but one of power, love, and a sound mind. Second, to my parents, who wanted me and loved me with the greatest capacity of human love that they could give. Third, to my spiritual fathers and mothers, Apostle Ernest Jordan and Lady Patricia Jordan, Drs. Carlton and Betty Wright, and Pastor Reuben and First Lady Nichole Lee for their love, encouragement, and laborious prayers for me to stand in who God says I am. Lastly, to my brothers, sons, and dearest friends, who believed I deserved to live and love abundantly.

Miracles and blessings,
Your daughter, sister, mother, and friend,
Loretta Everson

CONTENTS

FOREWORD

Sister Loretta comes from a family with rich biblical values and is no stranger to church. Her life became conditioned by abuse at an early age. Loretta learned how to mask hurt and pain as she developed into a successful woman, having received an education from the University of the Pacific, holding multiple degrees. She was promoted to and excelled as a human resources professional. She accomplished all this while surviving two abusive marriages, weathering through verbal, mental, and physical abuse.

When Loretta turned to God to deliver her, he did that and more. We have watched with amazement the wonders of God in her life, through the power of God, prayer, the Word of God, and the support of a strong spiritual family. It has been a great joy to see her development into the purpose God intended for her. She is now committed to sharing her story with women around the world in hopes that through the word of her testimony and the blood of the Lamb, victory can be brought to the broken.

Pastor Reuben and First Lady Nichole Lee
Hope Church and pastors at Stockton Tabernacle
of Faith, Stockton, California

INTRODUCTION

One of the most profound statements my father ever said to me was "Loretta, you are my daughter, my firstborn. I want you to never forget I loved and wanted you even before you were born. I will love you all your life. Don't ever forget that."

I was in the seventh grade when he said this to me. It was on a Saturday morning while I was riding in the car with him to Food Fair, our neighborhood grocery store, in Stockton, California. It was just an ordinary summer day, but that instance became one of the most profound moments in my life. Throughout my life my father would again randomly say this to me, which was endearing and heartbreaking at the same time. I would be a grown woman before I truly understood my emotions in those moments, not because my relationship with my father was broken but because I was broken in places neither he nor I could see.

When it comes to parents, I feel blessed and highly favored. My mother and father fell in love and married in a beautiful wedding ceremony on November 27, 1959. In fact, for years I fantasized about wearing a beautiful wedding dress someday like my mother did, my neck adorned with an elegant strand of pearls. I hoped to marry a man who loved and adored me the way my father loved and adored my mother. During the era I grew up, this did not seem like an impossibility. Fairy tales were meant to come true. I was born in the summer of 1965, just two days before my dad's birthday. I guess you could say I was his birthday present—at least that was his take on it.

The year I was born was controversial and ever changing. Having fought in the Korean War, my dad was preparing to get out of the Marine Corps. He had been wounded and awarded a Purple Heart. I am truly thankful for and proud of him. Other young fathers and young men were being drafted into the military service to fight a war in Vietnam that they didn't understand. Martin Luther King was fighting for African Americans' right to vote in elections. Malcolm X was assassinated for his political stance. Our streets were filled with hippies, black panthers, and riots. Singer Marvin Gaye was asking "What's Going On?" while Diana Ross and the Supremes were topping the music charts with the song "Stop! In the Name of Love," and the Beatles were belting out the song "Help!" So it came natural for me to think that I could change something in the world. Even if it was in a small part of the world, I wanted to leave my footprint. But it is hard to change what you don't understand, especially when your biggest puzzle is yourself. Before I could make any attempt to change the world, I would go on a roller-coaster ride of pain, setbacks, heartbreaks, and abuse. I would learn to embrace the ever-changing me—not the me that God created but the person the enemy of my soul tried to destroy. I would go on a journey that would ultimately teach me that my heavenly Father truly loved me and had a perfect and divine plan for my life that was much bigger than myself or my earthly father could ever dream of.

> *"For I know the plans I have for you," declares the Lord, "plans to prosper you and not to harm you, plans to give you hope and a future."* (Jeremiah 29:11 NLT)

A SPECIAL NOTE

I want to say a special thank you for taking the time to read my journey of turning pain into purpose and share with you my favorite scripture. This book contains journaled chronological accounts of my struggles with life and the battles that only God would help me triumph over. I realize that every one of us has a story, a heartbreak, and possible tragedy. This book is to show love and confirmation that you are not alone. I pray that these journaled experiences of mine will reach those who have experienced situations like mine or know someone who has. I pray that you can receive through my testimony the love of our heavenly Father and his power to break addictions, strongholds, depression, and insecurities, that you will know that he turns darkness into light. I pray blessings over your life as God reveals himself to you as you read, meditate, and reflect on this scripture and book.

Oh Lord, you have examined my heart and know everything about me. You know when I sit down or stand up. You know my thoughts even when I'm far away. You see me when I travel and when I rest at home. You know everything I do. You know what I am going to say even before I say it, Lord. You go before me and follow me. You place your hand of blessing on my head. Such knowledge is too wonderful for me, too great for me to understand.

I can never escape from your Spirit! I can never get away from your presence! If I go up to heaven, you are there; if I go down to the grave, you are there. If I ride the wings of the morning, if I dwell by the farthest oceans, even there your hand will guide me, and your strength will support me. I could ask the darkness to hide me and the light around me to become night—but even in darkness I cannot hide from you. To you the night shines as bright as day. Darkness and light are the same to you.

You made all the delicate, inner parts of my body and knit me together in my mother's womb. Thank you for making me so wonderfully complex! Your workmanship is marvelous—how well I know it. You watched me as I was being formed in utter seclusion as I was woven together in the dark of the womb. You saw me before I was born. Every day of my life was recorded in your book. Every moment was laid out before a single day had passed.

How precious are your thoughts about me, oh God, they cannot be numbered! I can't even count them; they outnumber the grains of sand! And when I wake up, you are still with me! (Psalm 139:1–18 NLT)

CHAPTER 1

Broke "N" Nightingale

I grew up in southeast Stockton, California, on Nightingale Street in a middle-class neighborhood with freshly cut green lawns and the sounds of children playing street games and hide-and-seek. There were two-parent families involved in the PTA, musicals, gymnastics, and sports. As kids we received constant guidance from our parents as they attempted to shape us into whom they desired us to be.

I can remember going to PTA meetings with my parents, the smell of freshly baked cookies with milk, and the feel of large, assorted crayons in my small hands with which to draw pictures that would be proudly displayed on the refrigerator at home.

I remember bike rides to the liquor store to get blue cream soda, Twinkies, and Lemonhead candy all for a dollar.

I remember the sound of skates with metal wheels rolling down the sidewalk and playing marbles in the gutter in front of our house.

I remember summer yard sales and bake sales with chocolate cupcakes, checkerboard cakes, and homemade snow cones and neighborhood birthday parties with homemade ice cream.

I remember Halloween candy, spooky costumes, and carving scary pumpkin faces lit up from the inside with candles and set out on the front porch.

I remember sitting on top of the car on hot summer nights at the motor movies with my dad, mom, and younger brother and sometimes my cousins on Friday nights.

I remember the smell of fresh buttered popcorn and hot dogs from Newberry's department store while shopping downtown with my parents.

I remember my backyard surrounded by yellow, pink, and purple roses and flutters of beautiful butterfly wings as I lay on the soft green grass looking up at clouds that resembled large, fluffy cotton balls shaped like sheep.

I remember hearing my uncle's beautiful Harley-Davidson motorcycle revving up as he gunned it, speeding past our house toward the neighborhood store. And I remember the sickening sound of my uncle's motorcycle crashing into the side of that neighborhood store just down the street from my house.

I remember running to the store and seeing blood and brains splattered everywhere, dripping down the store wall. I remember the sight of my great uncle's mangled body lying on the ground.

I can never forget that day, the day my uncle committed suicide.

It's amazing how a person can have thousands of wonderful memories of good things that happened in his or her life, and yet one bad thing can change everything. My uncle's suicide left me feeling confused and enlightened. There was no grief counselor to guide me. As a matter of fact, no one discussed the tragedy with me at all. After that I considered suicide an option when things got tough, a way out.

The thief comes only to steal and kill and destroy; I come that they may have life, and have it to the full. (John 10:10 NIV)

Having waited five years to have a child, my parents were overjoyed when I was born. Their love for each other was truly beautiful. My maternal grandfather was a minister, and my mom and siblings were raised in a loving Christian home rich with biblical values and thirteen brothers and sisters. My parents raised my brother and me in a Christian environment, which meant choir rehearsal on Tuesday evenings, prayer meetings on Thursday evenings, Sunday school and morning worship on Sundays, and Young People Willing Workers on Sunday evenings. We were taught the books of the Bible, the Ten Commandments, and that Jesus loved us and died for our sins. We learned that we could pray to the Lord and he would give us strength in any situation.

What I didn't learn or at least didn't understand in all those sermons is that the enemy of our souls begins attacking us through fear, disappointments, and childhood tragedies. He strategically devises plans to weaken and discourage our faith in God.

I truly thank God more than ever now for my parents and my Christian upbringing. And yet, although on the outside things looked good and felt good, the enemy had planted a detrimental seed in my heart that would later attempt to rule my life and destroy my future. Having received a bachelor's degree in liberal studies with a minor in child development, I now understand that from the moment a child is formed, all interactions and stimuli can have either a negative effect or a positive effect. The reality is that the environments we are exposed to become a part of our blueprint.

When I was a young girl, my mom worked as a typist while my dad was in the military. I was left with a family sitter in our neighborhood. Within that environment I was yelled out, hit, and deprived of food. Unfortunately I was too young to tell my parents what I was experiencing. My mom would jokingly say that when she would pick me up from the sitter's house, I would say in my toddler voice, "Hungry, Mama."

My mom thought it was so cute, never imagining that I hadn't been fed during the day. She just fed me. I used to overhear her mention that she sent groceries with me to the sitter's so she wondered why I was hungry all the time.

It is uncanny that the name of the street that I grew up on is named Nightingale because a nightingale is a passerine bird best known for its powerful and beautiful song. But it was on this street that my voice, my song, was silenced. My experience at the sitter's house on this street would hinder me from embracing the opportunities offered to me to develop without insecurities about what I could

3

do or become. It was because of the abuse and who inflicted it that I was unable to develop a healthy relationship with women in my life.

When my parents eventually found out about the neglect and abuse, my mother quit working and became a stay-at-home mom, and my father got out of the military. We never discussed the abuse, but I was never allowed to go to the sitter's house again.

I understand that prayer changes things, but families, especially Christian families, need to remember that talking about events and obtaining counseling is not a terrible thing. Family secrets have destroyed so many children's lives because even though the parents might have prayed about a situation, they never talked about it with their children.

My parents thought I was coping well, and since I seemed well adjusted, no counseling or treatment was offered to me. After all, they had prayed about the situation and moved on with their forgiveness. Unknowingly, they left me fractured and confused about love and relationships. But more important, I was hurting, fearful, and insecure. I got in many fights in grammar school because I was angry and I had learned how to fight back if I was harmed or mistreated.

What I didn't realize was that I wasn't just fighting a bully who laughed at me or hit me. I was fighting the effects of abuse by someone who should have been protecting me, someone I should have been able to trust. By the time I was in junior high school, the damage from my abuse began manifesting in a more dramatic fashion. I got in more fights and had my first occurrence of depression. In addition, my hormones were changing along with my emotions, and I was lost. My parents couldn't understand why when I walked into the house, I would seem to bring a dark cloud with me. My mom could not understand why I wasn't happy, and neither could I, so I isolated myself.

I was a good student and managed to be placed in the gifted program, but I was sad. One of my teachers wrote in the notes of my report card that I was *melancholy*. What a beautiful word for such a fractured countenance. The definition of *melancholy* in Webster's Dictionary is "a feeling of pensive sadness typically with no obvious cause." So in an effort not to make others uncomfortable, I learned quickly how to mask my feelings. In grammar school my anger and behavior got me in trouble with my parents, my teachers, and the principal. In junior high it interfered with my grades, so I became depressed, not understanding why I was angry. I had a root cause for my anger and depression, but I couldn't explain it. Since my personality made people uncomfortable around me, I learned quickly how to mask my feelings.

I had to find a way to control my anger and depression. This was the beginning of my battle with bulimia. I started my freshman year in high school in fear and spent my energy trying to do all the right things I was supposed to do in order to look well adjusted. I attended church faithfully with my parents, excelled in academics, participated in Camarata (the school choir), joined the track team, and made lots of friends. Yet I was attending a new school, meeting new people in a climate that was volatile due to schools desegregating. I was lost.

High school can be a cruel experience for many. Mean girls, jocks, popular kids, and smart, talented, and fractured human beings are being thrown into a melting pot. To be honest, I don't know how I survived but for the amazing grace of God. This is my journey of going from pain to purpose—my experiences with addiction, love, murder, tragedy, and heartbreak along with the biblical principles, miracles, and divine intervention that helped me overcome my past and embrace my future.

One of the biggest questions I had growing up was: Why did God allow me to be abused at such a young age? Why didn't he stop it? How could I be raised in a Christian home with praying parents and family and be hurt?

I understand that there are a plethora of abuse stories that trump mine. And I understand that during the time period that I grew up, efforts to avoid "sparing the rod and spoiling the child" meant beatings and whippings with switches, Hot Wheels tracks, shoes, wooden spoons, and anything else available at the time. We were told it was done out of love and according to biblical principles. It was a philosophy that worked for many families at the time. (If you openly disciplined this way now, you could end up in jail or worse!) I admit

I was not a stranger to a belt in my home, but I can truly say that my father did not physically discipline me. My dad left the disciplinary action to my mother.

I don't want to get into a political argument about corporal punishment, but back then the principal at your school could paddle you! However, receiving corporal punishment while being deprived of food, affection, or common kindness is a very different situation, especially when you are not old enough to understand what you did wrong. There is a struggle that comes with that type of experience. But seeing how I came from a Christian home with praying parents and family, it was hard to understand why God allowed me to suffer abuse. The truth for me is that God has nothing to do with people making choices to do evil, unloving things. God is love. God gives each person an opportunity to do good or evil. God did not create robots; we have free will to do good with what he entrusts us with or evil. We have a choice to do things our way or his way.

The first step in my healing process was to recognize that the abuse was not my responsibility; it was the abuser's responsibility. But my healing was the Lord's responsibility. In Luke 4:18 (KJV), Jesus says, "The spirit of the Lord is upon me, because he hath anointed me to preach the gospel to the poor, he hath sent me to heal the brokenhearted, to preach deliverance to the captives, and recovering of sight to the blind, to set at liberty them that are bruised."

I eventually forgave those who hurt me for not loving me, and I forgave myself for not loving me. I know that not loving myself may sound crazy to some people, but the truth is not loving yourself is a weapon the enemy uses to get you to not trust God. If the enemy can use circumstances to make you not love yourself, then how on earth can you trust God to love you? So I started the process to forgive myself for not loving but instead punishing and guarding myself. When we choose to utilize our own will to protect ourselves, we build a wall around our heart. That way no more hurt can get in, but no love gets in either. And the hurt we try to protect and guard gets nurtured and fed through destructive behaviors that can manifest through addiction, abuse, depression, and even suicide. All these are the enemy's playground. Some of us have so many layers of protection it's as if we had concrete and mortar around our hearts. Now that's what I call a *heavy heart*!

When we are wounded, we can encase and lock our hearts and then swallow the key. The blessing is that God knows how to get you to dispel the key. He knows everything about you, and he knows your combination. Genesis 1:31 says, "And God saw everything that he had made, and, behold, it was very good." Did you read that? Not just good but very good! I love Jesus's words in Matthew 10:29–31: "Are not two sparrows sold for a copper coin? And not one of them falls to the ground apart from your Father's will. But the very hairs on your head are full numbered. Do not fear therefore; you are of more value than any sparrows."

God knows us better than we know ourselves. As earthly parents, we love our children deeply and do our best to nurture and understand them, but not one human knows how many hairs are on another's head. There is a quote by Ethel Waters that says, "I am somebody because God don't make no junk." We must come to the realization that God made us, loves us, and has a purpose for us. God is proud of and pleased with everything he creates. We are his masterpieces. Our greatest challenge is to understand that there is a jealous, vengeful, evil, and calculating enemy who, as 1 Peter 5:8 says, "walks about the earth roaring like a lion, seeking whom he may devour."

The reason I say "calculating" is because for some of us the enemy starts when we are very young. The Lord has purposeful, loving thoughts and plans for us. He says, "For I know the thoughts that I think toward you, says the LORD, thoughts of peace and not of evil, to give you a future and a hope" (Jeremiah 29:11). But the enemy has a plan as well. Reverse the scripture to say the opposite: "The enemy knows the thoughts that he thinks for you, thoughts of discord and evil, to give you a horrible end." Thankfully God's promises trump anything the enemy has planned. Romans 8:28–29 says, "And we know that all things work together for good to those who love God, to those who are the called according to His purpose. For whom He foreknew, He also predestined to be conformed to the image of His Son, that he might be the firstborn of many brethren."

God's plan for us can never be deterred or thwarted because of the enemy's plans. Jesus suffered at the hands of evil men, and yet after enduring the cruelty of the cross, he conquered the grave. The enemy's plan did not work because God's plans are bigger than any evil the enemy can devise. God can turn all that the enemy means for evil into good. This is what happened to my favorite character in the Bible, Joseph.

Joseph said to his brothers, and I like to think to all who betrayed and hurt him, "Do not be afraid, for am I in the place of God. But as for you, you meant evil against me; but God meant it unto good" (Genesis 50:19–20).

Let's take a quick look at Joseph's life. "Now Israel [Jacob] loved Joseph more than all his children, because he was the son of his old age. Also he made him a tunic of many colors" (Genesis 37:3). Okay, so this starts off seemingly good for Joseph because he was favored by his father, right? This verse tells us he was loved, treated special, and, most of all, wanted by his father. It goes on to say that God gave Joseph a dream. How wonderful to be given a dream from God! How excited he must have been to tell his father and brothers. Even if he didn't understand the dream, he probably felt he could get support and clarification from his family, right?

But the enemy had a plan too. The enemy stirred up discord and jealousy in Joseph's brothers' hearts toward him. The enemy would turn their discord and jealousy into hate. Ultimately, the brothers would throw Joseph in a pit, sell him to a slave master, and take his coat and saturate it with goat's blood so they could trick their father into believing that Joseph had been killed. Joseph must have felt his circumstances were so unfair! He had done nothing to deserve such horrific treatment from his brothers.

Genesis 37:20 reveals how the enemy schemed to thwart God's plan with his evil plan. The brothers said, "Come therefore, let us now kill him and cast him into some pit; and we shall say, 'Some wild beast has devoured him.' We shall see what will come of his dreams!"

Look at how calculating the enemy is! Joseph's brothers eventually took advantage of the opportunity to sell him to the slave traders rather than kill him. I must take time to reveal God's intervention here. In one moment the brothers had conspired to kill Joseph, and in the next moment they agreed to sell him into slavery. As you read through this story in the Bible, notice that even during Joseph's crisis moments, the scripture says, "And the Lord was with him" (Genesis 39:2, 21).

Even though Joseph came from a loving, caring, God-fearing family, he had challenges from the enemy to overcome. Joseph's mother died when he was a child; his father played favorites, pitting him against his brothers; and Joseph had a bit of pride in who he was. After all, God gave him a dream of a high calling, and he was the preferred son of his doting father. But even after having received a purposeful dream from God, Joseph was thrown in a pit and later sold into slavery by his own brothers. Today this would be considered human trafficking.

Later on poor Joseph would be falsely accused of rape, convicted, and thrown into prison. In our society today, he would be considered a lost cause. His life would be ruined. Adding insult to injury, while in prison he interpreted the dreams of two prisoners, one of them being Pharaoh's chief butler, asking only one favor in return: "But remember me when it is well with you, and please show kindness to me; make mention of me to Pharaoh, and get me out of this house. For indeed I was stolen away from the land of the Hebrews; and also I have done nothing here that they should put me into the dungeon" (Genesis 40:14–15). Sadly the scriptures say, "Yet the chief butler did not remember Joseph, but forgot him."

This story is so powerful! There is acknowledgment of the divinity and sovereignty of God, an amazing example of forgiveness, and the revelation of God's beautiful plan. Ultimately, God's plan, Joseph's dream, came to fruition. And the Lord blessed Joseph to be fruitful in the land of his affliction and enabled him to forgive those who trespassed against him. In the end God's plan prevailed.

Do bad things happen to good people? The answer is yes. And do bad things happen to God's people? The answer is yes. We live in a world where people are freely making good choices and bad choices. Murder, abuse, rape, and cruelty will never be okay; but the enemy continues to convince people to make those types of evil choices.

God is revealing to us in this story that other people's bad decisions don't have to cripple us if we trust him with our lives. He knows this world is corrupt, but he is the light. God wants us to draw near to him, not just during the good times but also through tragedy, heartbreak, and betrayal. He wants us to be free to love, trust, and obey him, free to walk out his plan for our lives.

There are so many hurting adults who are actually still that mistreated child living in a grown-up body. I am amazed at how many of these adults are sitting, working, singing, teaching, ministering, and worshipping in churches still holding on to their past pain, not trusting God with their hearts even though they could be healed and help others like them. I know because I was one of them, and I found out I was not alone. I learned something profound about the heart as I began my journey of healing.

1 Samuel 16:7 says, "For the Lord does not see as man sees; for man looks at the outward appearance, but the Lord looks at the heart." Proverbs 4:23 instructs us to "Keep your heart with all diligence, for out of it spring the issues of life." To *keep* is to manage. Managing is an ongoing process; you are processing new information and managing the information all the time. Apostle Jordan, my spiritual mentor, taught me a valuable mantra to avoid what I call spiritual heart attacks: "Keep short accounts." This means when you are processing things through your heart, you don't hold things in. Holding things in causes clogged spiritual arteries.

Holding on to the memory's bad situations, hurts, betrayals, grief, and misunderstandings hinders us so that we are unable to hear God clearly. Our hearts should always be conduits for love. Our hearts are the most precious part of us to God. It is our core, our compass. The enemy is aware of this, which is why the enemy strategizes to bring about situations that will impact our hearts negatively. God wants us to give our hearts to him and to manage them by constantly flushing out the junk. The process of keeping short accounts is to take inventory, forgive, and let go. This process should occur all day every day. Letting go means releasing things that hurt us and giving them to God. The moment you realize that something has hurt you, even if it is a past childhood hurt, you must release it to God so the healing can begin. Keeping short accounts is one of the healthiest processes we can do in our lives. It gives us freedom to live an abundant life. Holding on to the enemy's negative pollutants in our heart clogs our heart. It does the one thing God wants to prevent. It takes away our ability to give God's love to others or receive love from others. It hinders us from loving ourselves, loving God completely, and receiving God's love, which is the greatest love of all.

Love is dependent on forgiveness just as forgiveness is dependent on love. In the Sermon on the Mount in Matthew 6:14–15, Jesus was very clear in his teaching about forgiveness. He said, "For if you forgive men their trespasses, your heavenly Father will also forgive you. But if you do not forgive men their trespasses, neither will your Father forgive your trespasses."

Wow! Now those are powerful words from Jesus himself. That means molestation, rape, spousal or child abuse, murder, and all other sins that may come against you must be forgiven. Sadly, many people haven't forgiven people who are dead. But there is hope if you are still living, breathing, and reading this book. You are in a position for God to do a miraculous healing of your heart if you want it. My heartfelt prayer is that you forgive and receive God's forgiveness to live a life free of pain and full of God's love.

In God's love, please pray with me:

Precious Father in heaven,

I come to you in Jesus's name. You in your great love sent your Son to earth to endure pain and suffering so that I could be forgiven. I now understand how important forgiveness is to you and for me. I ask you to heal my heart as I release everyone who has hurt me, and I forgive them just as you have freely forgiven me. Thank you for your love, grace, and mercy.

In Jesus's holy name,
Amen.

You were running a good race. Who cut in on you to keep you from obeying the truth? That kind of persuasion does not come from the one who calls you. "A little yeast works through the whole batch of dough." I am confident in the Lord that you will take no other view. The one who is throwing you into confusion, whoever that may be, will have to pay the penalty. (Galatians 5:7 NIV)

The Sprinter

Practice is the hardest part when you are off to a brand-new start.
You stretch and you run, but it isn't very much fun.
After you've finished practice and you think
you've gone through the worst,
just wait till you get home. Surprise! You've got a charley horse.
You toss and you turn and wince and even cry,
hoping the horrible night of pain will go by.
Tomorrow you say to yourself, "I'm going to start out fresh,"
but after the coach gets through with you, you feel like a mess.
Soon it's time for your first track meet,
and all you can feel is a strange tingling in your feet.
You hear the announcer call, "All runners, to your mark!"
So you set yourself in your block to start.
Then you hear the gun go off with a very loud bang!
And you wonder to yourself, *Am I going to be able to hang?*
Your legs are moving very fast trying to keep the pace,
hoping you will be the one to win the coveted race.
Then you feel that wonderful tape clinging to your chest.
But all you can think about is where to go and rest.
People say, "Did you hear us cheer?"
You say yes, but you really didn't hear.
All you heard was the rhythm of the other race mates' feet
and the very loud pounding of your own heartbeat.
This is all part of the joy for an athletic boy or girl.
There is joy in winning, and that feeling will remain.
But losing has its good points too. Participation
and teamwork are where you gain.

Loretta Young, 1983

13

CHAPTER 2

Running on Empty

Like most mothers from her era, my mother was an excellent cook and baker. She could make meals with very few ingredients and enjoyed every minute of it. How many mothers do you know who can make homemade donuts and apple turnovers?

Consequently, there were no missed meals in our home. And at suppertime, as my dad called it, we ate at the dining room table as a family. I loved my mother's cooking and tried to learn as much as I could from her. I love to bake and decorate cakes and cookies because of her love of cooking.

But I had a secret, a secret that made me feel good about myself and gave me control. Imagine sitting at the dinner table with your family eating a juicy, fried pork chop, smothered potatoes, green beans with bacon, a soft buttered roll, and pound cake for dessert. Now imagine having eaten as little of the meal as possible without anyone catching on, your stomach hurting, and your mind racing with all-consuming thoughts of when you can get to the bathroom alone in peace to throw it all up. That was me.

Most of the time, I would have to wait until my parents went to the den to watch television after nine to make sure the coast was clear. At other times it would be one or two in the morning that I would quietly slip into the bathroom, stick my finger down my throat as far as I could, and get rid of everything I could within my stomach.

Webster's Dictionary defines *bulimia nervosa* as "an emotional disorder involving the distortion of body image and an obsessive desire to lose weight, in which bouts of extreme overeating are followed by depression and self-induced vomiting, purging, or fasting." My battle with bulimia started my freshman year in high school. The triggers for me were a change in schools, a change in hormones, leaving my brother behind, and, hardest for me, meeting new people. The year I was set to go to high school, a rezoning law was approved, and my junior high was split into three districts. This was supposed to help desegregate schools, but it also resulted in race riots at my high school. I was terrified. The friends whom I had gotten close to for two years were sent to other high schools, and the relationships I had carefully built slowly withered.

It was easy getting into my studies, but it was still a transition, and two things I hated were allowing people get close to me and transition. I am by nature an introverted person; interaction with new people would drain me like an overused battery. I needed time to process and recharge, but in high school, there was no time for that. Figuratively speaking, it was sink or swim, and I was taught not only to swim but to also do the backstroke. Excelling was my only option, and I worked hard not to disappoint my parents.

So I was thrust into the high school melting pot of mean girls, jocks, popular kids, and highly academic students with neither the time nor the tools to figure out how to navigate through my emotions. To make matters more complicated, I was trying to balance my bulimia addiction with my new life. Bulimia is symbolic to purging. *Purging* is just a nice word for vomiting, but the word *purge* has relevance for me.

To *purge* is defined as "getting rid of whatever is impure and unwanted, to free oneself of the undesirable." I realized later in life that I was throwing up my insecurity, fear, and pain. I enjoyed the fact that I could control my weight and still eat whatever I wanted, but purging was not a means of weight loss for me. I was five feet and six inches tall and weighed 120 pounds, which is considered lean by body mass index standards. My physical weight was controlled by one of my favorite parts of high school, extracurricular activities.

There were three extracurricular activities that I loved and poured my heart and soul into: the track team, poetry team, and school choir. By the spring of my freshman year of high school, I had "mastered" my eating disorder and graduated to eating a round eight-inch white cake topped with buttercream frosting! I had a favorite bakery that I would go to where I would order a birthday cake decorated with pink flowers and with the words *Happy Birthday* written on it, partly because I was embarrassed and wanted to make it look as if it were for someone else and partly because it made me feel good. It seemed like a good way to celebrate my empowerment and to control my life. Even today I am still partial to a white cake with buttercream frosting smeared on top. I would go through all that trouble just to throw it all up.

The spring of my freshman year gave me the opportunity to have my first positive experience in high school, which was joining the track team. Sprint tryouts were held to test where you would fit in on the team. I chose sprints because the kids in my neighborhood always said I was fast. I had won my fair share of neighborhood street races, so I felt it was worth trying out. I must admit that I was surprised when I won the sprint race and was placed on the sprint 440 relay team. I was also positioned to race in the 100-meter and 200-meter runners groups. I was given the honor of becoming a female letterman, which was huge for a freshman. This honor immediately put me in the so-called "popular" crowd, which meant nothing to me but more pressure.

My parents were excited for me and bought me a beautiful green-and-gold letterman jacket that had my name and school mascot, the yellow jacket embroidered on the back. It was beautiful, and I was proud to wear it. My dad was a letterman in basketball in high school, and I was happy to make him proud as well. My freshman, sophomore, and junior years in high school were full of successes. I was featured in the Stockton *Record* newspaper for being selected as "black teenager of the year" by the Stockton Black Teachers Alliance for my academic achievements for writing, for winning races with my track team, and for going on tour with the school choir, "Camarata."

My mask seemed to work well for me. However, my senior year in high school was both confusing and disappointing both for me and for my parents. It was so bad that when my mom signed my senior memories book under "Parents' Thoughts," she wrote, "Don't blame me. I tried" (smile). My dad wrote, "I never really understood why you couldn't understand me. I hope someday you will, and soon."

To their credit, my parents did their best. They were loving and supportive Christian parents. Listen. I was featured in the newspaper for my academic achievements, I was on track to graduate high school, I had been accepted to San Diego State University, and I was still a virgin. I imagine that for the 1980s, based on societal barely-middle-class expectations, they did a great job. But between my fractured emotions, puberty, thoughts of transitioning from high school to college and being away from home, and my bulimia, I was in a daily state of terror. I felt as if I had reverted to being that hurt little girl again. I went into a depressed state of mind.

My bulimia was causing me to have nosebleeds and fainting spells. Running track became too strenuous, and I would pass out during races. My muscles cramped, pulled, and ached terribly, resulting in my quitting the team. It became so bad that my mom took me to the doctor and I was diagnosed with anemia. She was so glad that it was not sickle cell anemia, which ran in her family and took the life of at least one of my cousins and affected several others, that she didn't think to ask if anything else could be the cause. My mom and doctor's solution was to supplement more iron in my diet. I still remember the horror of eating fried liver, canned spinach, and rice once a week. Yuck!

By the time graduation rolled around, the combination of bulimia and anemia was debilitating for me. I remember my mom telling me that I carried a dark cloud with me. My dream after graduating high school was to graduate from the University of the Pacific with a bachelor's degree in the field of education, celebrate my accomplishment with a vacation in Hawaii, marry my prince charming, and have five sons and a career. My mom had put the idea of Hawaii in my head because she really wanted my dad to be stationed there so they could live there. However, even though my dad went to Hawaii in the Marine Corps, he never got stationed there.

Nonetheless, all those dreams failed to come to fruition because I was experiencing so much confusion and such an intense level of pain that it was debilitating and crippling emotionally. I wanted to be like my friends who were excited about leaving home, but I was terrified of leaving home and my parents. I knew I didn't have the tools to make it on my own. I went through the motions and got accepted to San Diego State University, which my cousin and I planned to attend together.

My parents were so excited that my dad took me to a car lot to buy me a car for college. He admitted that he envisioned seeing me go away to San Diego for college driving down the southern coast in a little convertible. My dad had been stationed in San Diego at Camp Pendleton while in the Marine Corps. He described to me how beautiful the coast was with its sandy beaches, clear blue skies, and the amazing ocean. He told me how he would run with his platoon on the coastal beaches.

It really sounded so beautiful, and yet I broke his heart by not wanting either of those things. I was too paralyzed with fear to go away from home, and I didn't want the car if it meant I had to leave home. My mentality was stunted; I was too afraid and honestly didn't understand why. My dad was angry and disappointed; consequently, he never bought me a car. What he didn't understand was that something was very wrong with me, but I was not capable of talking to my parents about what I was feeling. How could I articulate my emotions, feelings that I didn't understand myself?

So I stayed at home and went through the motions of evolving into a young adult. I enrolled in junior college, joined the track team, watched my close friends and schoolmates go away to college, and struggled with insecurity, addiction, and shame. I had dreams, but I was too confused to initiate them and too scared to believe in them. My entire teenage life I had been running on empty. No matter how many achievements or how much love I received, I had a hole inside my heart that seemed to never get filled. No accomplishment or promise could fill the emptiness that enveloped my life, but I was determined to survive, and so I developed my first mask. I felt if I could keep the outside looking okay, no one would see my inside. I would make myself up and "become" a person that people thought was normal.

It seems that since the beginning of time makeup has been used to cover up flaws. Women throughout history have put their health at risk, using many different types of homemade cosmetics. Women have used makeup to cover up what is really "them," from scars to pigmentation. Makeup is just an outer mask to hide perceived imperfections and insecurities or to enhance what is already there—to look perfect. There are a plethora of masks that can be used to hide the real you. I imagine that is why Halloween is a billion-dollar commercial holiday. But I'm not going to discuss outer masks or makeup.

No one really talks about emotional masks. These masks are the ones we hide behind because of fear, pain, disappointment, and childhood trauma. Fear produces insecurity. And insecurity can cause us to hide behind the masks of anger, status, false pretense, addiction, and control. My mask was control, but I could only mask so much before it all began to unravel.

God would begin to show me how to release that control to him through a roller coaster of events. I take great comfort now knowing that in the Word of God, it says, "For God has not given us a spirit of fear, but of power and of love and of a sound mind" (2 Timothy 1:7). It is not the desire of God that we live crippled by fear. The only fear that is healthy is the fear of not pleasing God. When I think about fear, I can't help but think of Elijah the prophet. You can't have faith and fear at the same time; that's a fact. Having faith in God requires faith and trust. I know from firsthand experience that when you are betrayed or threatened, faith and trust are hard to grasp. I am always amazed at how we as humans can accept great achievements, accolades, and blessings because of God's mercy and grace but not be fully capable of trusting or having complete faith in God when it comes to life's struggles.

In the Bible we read about Elijah and the many miracles God performed through him, but I want to talk about the miracles God did *for* Elijah. As an athlete who ran track, it intrigues me to read about Elijah's miracles. God enabled Elijah to run eighty miles to escape his fear. How far have you run in fear to escape pain or death? Spiritually, we run by utilizing our own methods to protect ourselves. Addictions like alcohol, drugs, sex, food, overspending, and even bulimia all are things we can use to get control, protect ourselves, or run from fear without seeking God.

Eventually Elijah got tired of running. When he was at his wits' end, having exhausted all his resources, God stepped in with *his* resources to strengthen and nurture Elijah. When Elijah was exhausted and thought his life was over, God provided shade for Elijah to rest. When Elijah was hungry, God sent a raven to provide him with meat and bread. When Elijah was thirsty, God provided a brook to drink from. The Lord was in control of Elijah's situation all the time. Our fears should lead us to the Lord, not to our own devices. The enemy of our souls has a plethora of substances and ideas to derail us from giving control of our lives to the Lord, who can provide all we need according to his riches in glory (Philippians 4:19). If we run to the Lord, we can be confident that his resources are never depleted! His hands are never empty of a solution to our circumstances. Even when we don't see it or understand it, he sees all and knows all things. God is the alpha and omega, the beginning and the end. Will you pray this prayer with me?

Precious Father in heaven,

I thank you for your goodness, mercy, love, grace, and provision. I ask that you forgive me in every area that I have not released control of my life to you. Any addiction that I have been using to sub-stitute releasing control to you, I release to you now. I ask that you heal my heart, which is so precious to you, and pray that you would "create in me a clean heart, Oh God, and renew a right spirit in me. Do not cast me away from Your presence, and do not take Your Holy Spirit from me. Restore to me the joy of Your salvation, and uphold me by Your generous Spirit" (Psalm 51:10–12).

In Jesus's holy name,
Amen.

CHAPTER 3

This Is No Laughing Matter

After enrolling in junior college, I got a part-time job close to home. This was a requirement to live at home with my parents. I complied because it was safe and comfortable. Those years were very confusing because I didn't really know what I wanted for my future. The truth was that I wanted a "do-over." I desperately needed a second chance. I joined the track team and started taking classes with a major in education. It was rough because I was in and out of depression, suffering from anemia, struggling with bulimia, and, for the first time in my academic career, failing. I used track as motivation to stay in school, but I was often so sick that I didn't perform well. I would faint during races, and my depression increased. In my second year running track, I injured my knee, resulting in surgery and ultimately ending my athletic endeavors. My weight dropped to 105 pounds, and I focused on work and school as much as I could.

In fact, I became obsessed with school. I would continue to take college courses, partly to boost my self-esteem. In my heart I desired to go to the University of the Pacific and get my bachelor's degree. I would ultimately go to college on and off from 1983 through 2013. Yes, you read that correctly. It took me thirty years! By the time I finished going to junior college, I had received five associate degrees! I held degrees in sociology, religion, early childhood education, liberal arts, and social science. And in 2013 my dream came to fruition; I graduated from the University of the Pacific with a Bachelor of Arts in liberal studies with a minor in early childhood education and a specialization in special education autism spectrum, cum laude. It took me thirty years to accomplish what most people accomplish in four! This became a running joke among my family and friends, but it did not deter me because no one understood the internal and external struggles that I dealt with for the incredible journey.

Now I don't want you to think that their cynicism and jokes did not hurt; they did. But they also gave me motivation to complete what I started. Going to college and seeing my dream come to fruition gave me hope and purpose while I was so fractured emotionally. But no matter how many classes I took or degrees I acquired, I was empty inside and extremely insecure. So I turned my thoughts to relationships to fill my emptiness. When you are raised in a home with parents who had a fairy-tale wedding, who are still married and following biblical principles, you tend to fantasize that all of what they had you can have too. I was taught biblical scriptures like "it's better to marry than to burn" and "what God has put together let no man put asunder." I believed that all marriages consisted of white wedding dresses with veils and tuxedos and churches. This may seem naïve, but I believed there was a prince charming out there somewhere just for me.

My reality would be terribly different than anything I had ever known. My parents tried hard to shelter me. I wasn't allowed to go on a date with anyone until I was sixteen years old. In fact my first date was chaperoned by my parents. It started with him and me sitting with my parents at my brother's high school football game. After the game he drove me to Eddie's pizza parlor, which was one block away. My parents and brother met us there. And we ate pizza, talked, and played video games. My parents allowed him to drive me home. And, yes, he had a car, which was great. He was also smart and handsome. On this night I would experience my first kiss. I was in love, well, puppy love. I considered this guy my first boyfriend, but I really didn't understand relationships or stay in one long enough to learn how to navigate the relationship because I was emotionally crippled. It looked like immaturity but in reality was a mask to cover my fear.

It took too much energy for me to hide my insecurities from a person so close to me. So my first boyfriend relationship ended, and I was confused at why and how. Most of my relationships ended with me giving up because it was just too hard to mask my pain.

My second significant relationship could be classified as my "first love" or, as Prince Charles famously stated when asked about love, "whatever love actually is." I was introduced to a young man by his brother while I was standing at the bus stop on Nightingale Street. It was such an interesting experience. His brother drove past me, then backed up his car, parked, and got out. I was a little afraid because he was wearing a correctional uniform, and I don't think I had seen that type of uniform before; he looked like a sheriff. Nonetheless he politely approached me and asked if I was single. Hesitantly I replied "yes." He then asked if I would like to meet his younger brother and explained that his brother had just moved to Stockton from Oakland, California, and didn't really know anyone.

I was flattered and very intrigued at this point. This may sound a bit corny for this date and era, but it was in the 1980s. People had a very different mentality than now; we talked to one another face-to-face. I felt it must be fate and was intrigued because he was not from Stockton. Our first date was arranged, and we quickly connected. This was the start of my first real experience with love. As we became closer, I introduced him to my parents, and he was willing to begin attending church with me. By fall of our first year dating, we were engaged to be married. He did everything right in my eyes. He got down on one knee and asked me to marry him while holding the most beautiful ring I had ever seen. Prior to asking me, he had already gotten my parents' blessing, and they were thrilled. They had come to love him like a son.

I was so excited about seeing my fairy tale come to fruition, but the stress of a wedding overwhelmed me, and fear gripped my heart as it had in high school before graduation. Unfortunately, before my maid of honor and bridesmaids could even finish paying for their dresses, the wedding was off and the relationship painfully over. I had called off the wedding and the relationship. Although I was disappointed in myself, I knew I had done the right thing. I got over it quickly because I was not capable of loving him or anyone else for that matter. He was an amazing man and had a great vision for his future. But when he told me his dreams, I became terrified because I knew it was impossible for me to be part of them. We parted ways amicably, and I masked my disappointment and confusion with another relationship.

> *"Fear not; you will no longer live in shame. Don't be afraid; there is no more disgrace for you. You will no longer remember the shame of your youth and the sorrows of your widowhood anymore. For your Creator will be your husband, the Lord of Heaven's Armies is his name! He is your Redeemer, the Holy One of Israel, the God of all the earth. For the Lord has called you from your grief—as though you were a young wife abandoned by her husband," says your God. "For a brief moment I abandoned you, but with great compassion I will take you back. In a burst of anger I turned my face away for a little while. But with everlasting love I will have compassion on you," says the LORD, your Redeemer.*

These words from God give great comfort to all of us who have fallen into a dark place in our lives. During those moments when we are rejected and neglected—even when it is a result of our own doing—God still remembers us. His love endures despite our failures because there is no failure in him. When he seems distant, we must always remember that he is closer than we think. God is waiting with loving, open arms to give us a good ending to our story.

Please, let me agree with you in prayer:

Precious Father in heaven,

We come in agreement in prayer with thanksgiving, praise, glory, and honor. We ask you to forgive us. We ask for your forgiveness so we may be free to come to you in love and grace. Romans 8:1 says, "There is therefore now no condemnation to those who are in Christ Jesus, who do not walk according the flesh, but according to the Spirit." We also forgive ourselves and everyone involved and trust you to forgive our sins and heal our hearts, minds, and souls.

In Jesus's holy name,
Amen.

I have many reasons to live, but I want to die because the reasons for me to live break my heart and make me cry. Breathing, sleeping, and focusing are hard for me. My mind races and I can't catch up; my body paces and I throw up. I am empty and broken. My soul cries; my tears run. I have nothing more to give. I have many reasons to live, but I want to die because the reasons for me to live break my heart and make me cry. (LGY 2006)

CHAPTER 4

What God Has Put Together

Tina Turner had a hit song called "What's Love Got to Do with It?" I can relate to that song. After a series of unfruitful relationships, I had made up my mind that I needed to get married. Being an unwed mother was not the best life, and the truth is I was tired of embarrassing and hurting myself and my family. So my wish to get married wasn't about being in love as much as it was to save face. I wanted to move on and cover up an embarrassing situation with an act I thought would make my situation respectable. In my experience that meant getting married. My son was a year old when I met my first husband. I'm not sure if he was really attracted to me or to my being fractured. After all, he had witnessed firsthand the betrayal and humiliation I went through in my last relationship because his brother happened to be the best friend of my son's father. Yes, you read correctly. Birds of a feather seem to really flock together.

Within three months after meeting, we were married. It was not a whirlwind romance. It was a marriage of convenience, opportunity, and 100 percent pride on my part. I believed it would assuage my parents' disappointment and ease their embarrassment within the Christian community. It was the only way I knew to regain some respect and get revenge at the same time. The roses the young man brought to my job once a week, the long rides up the coast on weekends, the nice dinner dates, and his patience with my son were the perfect remedy for me to escape the humiliation I had endured. I had come back to the Lord, and he was a churchgoing man. It seemed like a good fit at the time. It didn't matter that I didn't know how to love because I didn't love myself or that people were against the union. I wanted and needed to end this feeling of emptiness that I continued to carry.

In essence, I masked my fractured emotions with a marriage to a man I didn't know how to love. Deep down in my broken heart, I knew I was making this decision out of shame, hurt, and revenge. But my pride told me it was worth taking the chance. I was willing to bet my life on a marriage that had no foundation. That being said, the price of trying to save face would be more than I could afford to pay. I began enduring a cycle of abuse that I would struggle with for the next twenty-five years! I would survive being pushed out of a moving car, thrown through a car window, and choked until I passed out. I also suffered a broken arm and a broken nose. I've been slapped, kicked, headbutted in the face, pinned down to a bed, and suffocated with a peanut butter sandwich to quiet my screams and endured numerous other atrocities that are baffling to me even now. All that may seem incomprehensible for any sane person to endure, yet I felt I was strong enough to persevere. I now understand that no matter how strong or determined one is to make things work in an abusive situation, there will come a breaking point, and that point will either make you or break you.

For me it would happen at the five-year mark of our marriage. By this time, I had two young sons whom I loved dearly. I was working and going to school, hoping to somehow make a better life for us. I lived in a bubble, going to church and pretending to be okay, but it wasn't working. My husband would go to church and participate, but he relapsed into alcoholism. He was mean and cruel, and I was cold and distant. The hoax was up, and we both felt unloved and trapped in a cycle of abuse and pain. I didn't know what to do, but I knew that I didn't want to be a single mother again, especially with two children. So I purposed in my broken heart that I would do my best to make it work by tolerating whatever my husband brought my way. We were living a lie. We would attend church faithfully. And I would endure the verbal and physical abuse, alcoholism, and loneliness. That being said, there was one thing I had no tolerance for, and that was infidelity.

My husband was close to his coworkers and played on the company softball team. It became our family pastime, and all the wives and husbands grew very close. His coworkers and their families became our surrogate family. We shared our children's accomplishments, date nights, holidays, parties, and game night rituals. Between annual company picnics, Christmas parties, weddings, and new babies added to the fold, we had become a close-knit group of friends.

At this five-year mark of our marriage, my husband began going to softball games without my sons and me, at first because our sons had started playing sports and we would divide our time supporting them. But eventually I realized he was purposely excluding me from the games. He was coming home later and later. On weekends he either had tournaments or made plans with out-of-town family and friends, excluding me and the children.

By this time, we had a total of four sons together: his two sons from a previous marriage, my son, and our youngest son we had together. He would leave for his court-ordered visitation weekends with his older sons and not come home at night, leaving me with the children. I didn't mind spending time with all the boys; they were great together. But eventually my radar went up, and I started asking him questions. Instead of answers, I received acute verbal abuse, which made me feel even more suspicious and insecure. These arguments would always result in him leaving for longer periods of time. After a while, my husband stopped coming home on weekends altogether.

This behavior began in November, and by May he was involved in a full-blown affair. His behavior took a toll on my already fragile emotions, but it was when I witnessed it for myself that I truly broke into pieces.

I had vented to one of his coworkers' wife, who was a pretty good friend. We had been witnesses at their wedding and spent a lot of time together. Out of the blue one evening, she phoned me, telling me that I really needed to get to the company softball game because she couldn't keep my husband's affair from me, despite her husband telling her to stay out of it. I happened to have all the boys that evening, so I quickly arranged for a babysitter and drove to my husband's game without his knowledge. My friend wanted me to see for myself exactly why he was excluding me. Now, I can't speak for any other woman but myself, but I had such an intense desire to see his mistress's face. I had an insatiable need to compare, talk to, and confront her. But it was the most heartbreaking experience I have ever felt in my life besides the death of a family member. You can't imagine the feeling of going to your husband's company softball game and seeing his mistress at the other end of the bleachers looking at him with pride and affection. The worst part is that everyone knew but me because he had been taking her to his games for a while.

When I got to the ballpark, I felt a familiar sense of pain and betrayal, the anguish I had masked before by marrying my husband. This familiar pain he was inflicting caused my mask to fall, and somehow my legs moved without my help or recognition. I approached the bleachers looking for an unfamiliar face. My friend motioned for me to come sit next to her, and she discreetly pointed out the other woman. I sat calmly studying the woman's face, her expressions, and the look of adoration toward my husband, her boyfriend. She was pretty and young and seemed very sweet from a distance.

My husband, not expecting me to be there, did not notice me in the stands. Strangely, I didn't feel angry or nervous. I sat for a moment processing the entire situation and assessing my emotions. I didn't feel angry. *Why was that? Did I expect this to happen? Did I not love him?*

Then I forcefully directed my focus back to the other woman. *It isn't her fault*, I told myself. *She doesn't know he is married.* I decided since my husband was keeping the secret, it was my duty to expose him. I approached the woman as quietly and respectfully as I could. As I sat next to her, I felt empowered and asked her whom she was there to see on the softball team. She politely said my husband's name with a loving schoolgirl giddiness, as if she had won a prize.

For a moment I felt compassion for her. New love is such a beautiful feeling. I thought about the times I felt my first kiss or attraction and was reminded of what a nightmare it could turn out to be. I asked her what her name was because for some reason I needed to know that information for my memory bank of his transgressions. I then introduced myself by telling her my first and last name. And then with complete disgust, I heard myself say, "His wife."

There was no pride or adoration when I said it, nor was there any anger. I proceeded to tell her that she should get a ride home because things weren't going to go well. I had planned to confront him, and then he and I would exit the park together. Leaving her there without any explanation from him was not meant to hurt her; it was meant to hurt him and expose him.

It felt as if I were playing a part in a movie. I then stood up and took one good look at her. I wanted to remember her face forever. I needed this visual information for my memory bank as well.

She looked visibly frightened, with tears in her eyes. I remember thinking to myself, *Why is she crying?* And then I became angry, not at her but at him. I proceeded to second base where he was standing but not before grabbing a bat from the dugout. My egotistical, arrogant, abusive, philandering husband didn't even see me coming. Somehow, the bat was in swing mode, and I demanded he leave with me "now." My friend took my car to her house, and my husband surprisingly complied without issue. We drove in silence to pick up our sons from the babysitter, and it was even more silent as we drove home. Once we tucked the boys into bed, he turned into a verbally abusive, vicious, out-of-control monster.

It wasn't the first fight we had; it was one of many. But this fight had a different tone. It felt different and sounded different. When my husband left to go mend his mistress's broken heart, he was calm and cool; and before he closed the front door, he made sure to tell me that he did not love me anymore. Hearing the door close was weird; there was no slamming or disturbance. There was a finality to that moment as he closed the door behind himself.

I sat on the couch puzzled and empty, thinking about his declaration to me. It would have been a fair statement for him to make because I didn't love him from the start, but he said "anymore." This meant he either loved me at the start or fell in love at some point along the way, and for some reason that stung me. I was confused by his statement.

Should I forgive him and try to save my marriage? Was I capable of loving him? Could he love me again if I learned to love him? These questions raced around in my head and heart constantly. The longer I tried to rationalize my situation, the more I became unraveled. This time I couldn't find a mask to cover the pain. Somehow my mask had fallen. My heart was open. And every hurt, rejection, and betrayal all became one big infection that began spreading, encompassing my mind, my heart, and my soul.

I stumbled through the motions of life as if in a fog. I went to work until I couldn't work. Honestly, that week is still a mystery to me because I still can't remember the details. However, I do know that during that period I became the saddest and most desperate I had ever been in my life. In retrospect I can now see that the trigger of infidelity opened every wound I had covered up. I thought I wanted to fight for my marriage, but my soul was fighting for my life. I had spent years fighting hurt, disappointment, humiliation, and shame in my own strength. But I had finally run out of solutions, schemes, and ideas. I had come to a crossroads: do or die. It was here that I would see myself clearly. It was here that I would meet God. And it was here that I would truly understand just how fractured and broken I was.

CHAPTER 5

Live or Die

The following weekend my husband came home dressed in his company softball uniform. I thought he was coming to pick up the boys and me to go watch his game. Our sons didn't have any games, so we were free for the weekend. The boys were excited to see their dad and asked if they could go to the softball game with him.

He responded "no," and his response troubled me. I didn't understand why he did not want us to go with him, and I questioned him. An argument ensued between us, and before I knew it, my husband aggressively yanked me up from the ground I was standing on and threw me into the window at the back of my car. When he picked me up, my heart stopped beating for a split second. I thought he was going to kill me. My ears popped, and the sound of his yelling and cursing became muffled, as if we were in a tunnel. Then I heard glass shattering, and my heart started beating again. I rolled off the back of the car and felt my body hit the ground hard.

The next sound I heard was his car speeding out of the driveway. My eldest son—scared, confused, and yet relieved—helped me up and into the house. I was no longer fractured; I was completely broken. My body wasn't broken, just a few bumps and bruises, but my mind had somehow snapped. Within weeks I lost twenty pounds. I couldn't eat and quickly became emaciated. Yet I stayed and pretended to be okay, talking to no one—not even God. Still, despite all the pain and humiliation I had endured, nothing would prepare me for what would happen next.

It had been just about a month since my husband had stayed home overnight. His habit was to come home just long enough to get a change of clothes and leave. I finally got enough nerve to tell him that if he was going to continue to have an affair, we should get a divorce. He told me that was not an option and walked out the door, leaving me bewildered and without resolve.

All my carefully planned ways of running away from and masking the former pain and humiliation from my previous relationship were useless. I was right back where I started, humiliated and ashamed. That evening, I was desperate to free myself from the pain I was feeling. I wasn't sure if my heart was broken or the marriage was broken, but there was one thing I was sure of: I was broken. I took a couple of Xanax and put Toni Braxton's song "Unbreak My Heart" on repeat.

I could hear my sons in the yard laughing and playing. *I love them so much*, I thought to myself. They sounded very happy, so free. I wondered how they were so happy when their mother was in so much pain. I felt sorry for them because they had me as a mother. They deserved better, and I wanted to change what was happening to me so I could be better for them. I started self-talk, trying to rationalize what happened between my husband and me earlier in the day. I thought about my former relationship and the pain it had caused, how I was still ashamed of being a "baby mama." As I reflected on the rejection and humiliation I felt in the past, my heart was pierced, as if those moments were happening in real time. I thought about how I had disappointed my parents by not finishing school. I thought about my failed relationships. I thought about my abortion, and with each thought I took more pills.

I was getting sleepy. I could feel my eyes burning. I was mentally and physically exhausted. My body still ached from being thrown against the car window, and I longed for relief from the pain I felt internally and externally. I called the boys inside and gave them a snack while they watched television. Then after they had taken their baths, I went to each of their rooms to pray with them and tuck them in. I put the song "Unbreak My Heart" back on repeat and prepared myself a bubble bath.

I thought about the broken window in the car and its cost. I thought about my husband not being home, about him being with another woman. I thought about my life, my past, my present, my future. And I took a razor and cut my left wrist. There was very little blood because I didn't do it right, just like everything else in my life.

I needed to talk to someone. I was hurting too much inside to fix it myself this time; I was in trouble. But whom could I talk to who wouldn't judge me, ridicule me, or give me a lecture? I got out of the bath, wrapped my wrist in bandages, and decided to call the suicide hotline. As I was putting on my nightgown, I felt a little dizzy. I was tired, confused, and stuck. I figured the person on the suicide hotline would understand; they would give me some clarity—maybe even put the broken pieces of my heart back together again. I went to the kitchen to get a glass of water and grab the phone book to make my call. I marveled at how clean the kitchen was because I was teaching my sons how to mop the floor and wash dishes. I could smell the hint of bleach. I loved the smell of bleach in the kitchen and bathroom; somehow it represented cleanliness to me. My sons had done a good job despite me having poured Ajax all over the floor in frustration and displaced aggression.

I sat on the couch with the telephone book and opened it to the suicide hotline page. The advertisement read in bold lettering: "Suicide Prevention Hotline: The lifeline provides free and confidential support." The word *confidential* stuck out like a sore thumb, as my mother would say. I felt some relief. *Maybe they had a solution for my racing thoughts besides the ten Xanax I had just taken. Was it ten?*

I couldn't think straight. I felt assured that they would talk me into happiness again. I wanted to laugh again. I desperately wanted to be free of pain and worry. Then, before I could make the call, something strange happened. My mind started acting odd. It was as if my thoughts were separated into four areas and I was compartmentalizing everything I knew or experienced. The painful memories started playing a movie of my life. I could hear music faintly in the background of my racing thoughts. I had a strong desire to see my sons, but I couldn't walk.

I quickly dialed the hotline number; I needed help fast. A man answered, and I was relieved because I didn't want to talk to a woman for some odd reason that I didn't understand. The man said "hello" and gave me his name. He then asked me how I was doing and asked for my name.

I wanted to answer professionally in an upbeat manner. I wanted to explain my situation as if we were two friends having lunch together at a nice restaurant. Instead my words were slurred, and my thoughts were scrambled. My left wrist was still bleeding, and I panicked. He asked me if I had taken anything, and I told him yes.

He said they would send help. That is what I needed—help. Nonetheless, while the police were directing me into the back of the patrol car to transport me to the mental hospital, I could only watch as social services workers took my sons and put them in another car. I was crying hysterically, and so were they.

I had messed things up again. My thoughts were scrambled and unclear, but one thing was very clear to me: this was not help! When I arrived at the hospital, I was secured on a twenty-four-hour suicide watch, which meant I could have no contact with anyone inside or out. All they knew was that I had taken Xanax and attempted to slit my left wrist. They pumped my stomach. After sleeping from pure exhaustion, I woke up in a strange place desperately looking for my sons. I was released to my father-in-law because I did not want my parents to know what I had done. It wasn't until I was told that I could not immediately get custody of my children that I included my parents in my mess.

In fact, I was not even allowed to see my children. They had split my two sons up from one another. My eldest was in a children's home facility, and my youngest was in a foster home somewhere in Modesto. I knew in my heart that my sons were scared and alone, and I couldn't be there for them. I frantically called my brother to go get them, but authorities would not release custody of them to anyone until I went to court. I thank God that my mother-in-law was a licensed foster mother and was able to secure a home visit rather than having to wait for a court date. This was agreed to only because the children had not been harmed and our home was deemed a safe environment.

A "safe environment" meant the house had to be clean, with food in the cabinets and refrigerator and bedrooms fully equipped with furniture, blankets, toys, and pictures. My mother-in-law contacted my husband because social services stipulated that both parents needed to be present for the meeting.

My husband agreed to come home for the meeting with the social worker even though he was living with his mistress. I was freshly released from the mental health facility still on acute anxiety medication. We were broken, but we both put on masks that portrayed a loving, committed married couple who were doting parents, responsible, and stable. We put on a united front confirming that we would be the best parents for our children and that I would get the support I needed to provide a stable home for them. When the social worker left, so did my husband. I took two sleeping pills, hoping the nightmare would be over when I woke up.

The following day the social worker brought my sons home, and I cried, asking their forgiveness. The three of us sat on the couch hugging. While holding my sons in my arms, a flood of love and responsibility for them came over me. In that same moment, all worry, care, and concern for my husband's whereabouts or well-being left me completely.

The next day my uncle sent me three round-trip airplane tickets to Los Angeles. We stayed there for a month so I could heal and get my head together. My mom considered it to be an intervention to give me time and space to mend and gain a new outlook on my life. This time my mother took an active role in discussing what I was going through. She not only prayed about the situation but prayed me through the situation.

While we were in Los Angeles, my husband's mistress left him because she had gotten evidence from her grandmother, who knew his grandmother, that we were married and, in her words, "church ceremony, beautiful wedding dress, cake, and all." I am still puzzled at how my confrontation was not enough for his mistress to believe my husband was married. It was proof to me how desperate hurt women can be to believe a lie and accept a man who is clearly fractured into their lives. Maybe she was fractured too.

My husband contacted me, crying and begging for me to give our family another chance. He petitioned, pleaded, and promised to make life better for us. My pride wanted to believe him because I needed to save face. My fear wanted to believe him because I did not want to be a single mother again and now I was no longer fractured. I was completely broken and needed time to get myself together. So I went home. Our broken spirits agreed to live lives that masked verbal and physical abuse, disrespect, and unforgiveness for seven more years.

I was terrified of being a single mom again, so I kept taking college courses in order to get a better job. Although I worked, I was dependent on my husband's income to live. I honestly don't know how I survived, but I know the exact day I said, "No more!" My heart couldn't take another break. I was tired of pretending to be something that I was not. I could feel myself going into depression again. I had lost sixty pounds and was taking sleeping pills to get through my torment-filled nights. I had managed to graduate from junior college despite my nervous breakdown and broken marriage and had started preparing myself to leave. I had to file bankruptcy and save every penny. All I needed was time.

But while I was preparing for a new life, I learned my mother was fighting for her life. One beautiful spring day in May of 2003, my father contacted my brother and me requesting that we come over for dinner. Without reservation I went, excited to be together, just the four of us. After dinner we went out to the breakfast room and had some lighthearted conversation. Then without warning, my mom dropped a bombshell that changed the trajectory of all our lives. She had been diagnosed with leukemia and had less than a year to live.

It felt as if my heart had been ripped out of my chest. Every part of my body felt sick; I wanted to throw up. I began to cry and laid my head on her chest, and she held me in her arms. In that moment I wanted to be a little girl again. I wanted to go back in time and make more memories. I wanted to erase every misunderstanding and every time I hurt her with my poor decisions.

My dad pulled my brother and me close and said, "We have to be strong for your mother."

Before I left my parents' home, my mother gently whispered to me, "It's okay to cry, baby."

But Dad's voice was the one that echoed in my mind, stronger, louder, and clearer: "We have to be strong for your mother." This was no time to be a crybaby. I needed to be strong.

When I got in my car, something shut down in my heart. Something inside me stopped the tears from falling down my cheeks. No more crying about my abuse, my marriage, or disappointments— and no crying about my mom's diagnosis. Emotionally, I shut down completely that day.

I had to get my life together quickly because my support system was leaving this earth. I needed to be in control to help my parents and to be there for my mother every moment I could. I made a promise to myself that this would not cause me to lose control emotionally. Never again would I allow myself to be put in the mental hospital.

A week later my mom was hospitalized, and I was afraid it would be the last time I would see her. I had determined that I was not going to spend my mother's last days in a miserable, abusive, unloving relationship. I told her I was leaving my husband because his infidelity and abuse was too much, but I was fearful of raising my sons alone. My mom told me, "You won't be the first or the last woman to be a single mother. It's better to raise your sons in a safe home that an abusive home."

I took a half day off from work. While my husband was at his job and my sons were at basketball practice, I went home and packed a few things for my sons and me. I took only things that could fit in my car, like personal items and clothing. Unfortunately, my husband came home from work early. I don't know if someone told him or if it was coincidence, but I was determined to not let him change my mind.

I didn't think there could be anything worse than my husband throwing me through a car window. But no matter how scared I was of him, I felt positive that if I didn't leave, I would die. My husband was furious and attacked me, but I kept packing. He began to throw things at me, but the final straw for me was him throwing my pink bowling ball through my car window. I did the only thing I could do: run to a neighbor's home and call the police.

I didn't want to call the police. I didn't want to cause him harm; I just wanted to leave. It took five police cars to scare him enough to get him out of our home. He had barricaded himself in the house with his dogs at the door, and the police were apprehensive to go in because he had a gun. By the time the police managed to get into the house, he had escaped.

The police granted me a temporary restraining order against my husband, and I left our home with all I had in my car along with my two sons and my brokenness. I drove to the park to catch my breath and figure out where to go. Finally I called my father and told him what had transpired.

He responded with a strained voice, saying that he couldn't let me and my sons live with them because my mom's immune system was just too low. In the past his response would have hurt me, but I felt nothing but understanding. I had to be strong for my mother and not bring extra stress and burdens to their doorstep. I had to figure this out myself somehow.

My options were limited. I couldn't go to my in-laws for obvious reasons. My best friend's husband didn't want to get involved, nor did my brother. I have come to understand that marital issues become a very sticky area of understanding for most people, especially family. I don't have to name the numerous tragic incidents of families being imprisoned or murdered trying to support a loved one involved in an abusive relationship. I blame no one for doors that were closed.

But God opened a door. The mother of my eldest son's friend called me and offered for my sons and me to stay with them. Desperately and gratefully, I moved my family into her home. My youngest son and I slept together in a twin bed, and my eldest slept on the floor in the loft. The only thing that mattered to me was that my sons and I were safe. I will always be grateful to this amazing woman for the compassion and kindness she unselfishly showed us.

My sons and I quickly acclimated to our new environment. By the summer of that year (May 2003–July 2003), I was blessed to secure a fully furnished home to accommodate my sons and me as we concentrated on our well-being. I started school again and focused on my sons' academics and their extracurricular sports and my last days with my mother. I had survived what I thought was the worst part of my life.

When I reflect on my marriage, I know that I married out of pride and shame rather than love. At the time of my marriage, I considered myself to be a Christian, as did my husband. Prior to marriage we abstained from sex, went to church faithfully, and sought godly counsel. Yet God had said "no" to our marriage, once through his family pastor and once through my spiritual counselor. But our pride and wanting to do things our way overrode godly counsel. We disobediently married into a life of brokenness, heartbreak, addiction, abuse, and, ultimately for me, attempted suicide. It's been said that hurting people hurt people. Sadly, when it comes to marriage, two broken pieces don't make a whole. I didn't think a brokenhearted person could have pride. I learned that pride can come in many forms, and in my case it came in the form of protecting myself. Philippians 2:3 (NIV) says, "Do nothing out of selfish ambition or vain conceit. Rather, in humility value others above yourselves."

I don't think anyone wants to be in a loveless, abusive relationship or marriage. Our pride will do just about anything to survive physically and mentally. I believe this is one of the many reasons many people are addicted to alcohol, street drugs, and prescription pills even at the expense of their health and well-being. I have heard that self-preservation is the goal to ultimately achieve success in life, something I believed before I considered myself to be a Christian. But being a Christian is being Christlike. That means displaying the fruit of the spirit, which is love, joy, peace, patience, kindness, goodness, faithfulness, gentleness, and self-control.

This may seem like a tall order to fill all day every day. It takes trusting in God, not in ourselves or in any other person, to protect, heal, and preserve us. Romans 7:18–25 (ESV) says,

> *For I know that nothing good dwells in me, that is in my flesh. For I have the desire to do what is right but not the ability to carry it out. For I do not do the good I want, but the evil I do not want is what I keep doing, Now if I do what I do not want, it is no longer I who do it, but sin that dwells in me. So, I find it to be the law that when I want to do right, evil lies close at hand. For I delight in the law of God, in my inner being, but I see in my members another law waging war against the law of my mind and making me captive to the law of sin that dwells in my members. Wretched man that I am! Who will deliver me from this body of death? Thanks be to God through Jesus Christ our Lord! So then, I myself serve the law of God with my mind, but with my flesh I serve the law of sin.*

It became clear to me after dealing with the aftermath of my attempted suicide, divorce court, child custody battles, and having to pay spousal support that trying to right a wrong or fix myself takes more than willpower. If we know we can't change others, why do we continue to try? God is the only one who can change our brokenness into wholeness. We may try to change our outer appearance with a more attractive body or face and our status with a better job or higher education, but God can change your inner core. Your heart is his main concern. You can't heal a broken heart with physical methodology. A healed heart takes spiritual surgery, with God as the physician. It takes some time to heal after physical surgery; we must wait for the process to be complete. It is the same principle with spiritual surgery. God had me open on the surgery table, my heart exposed, and it was there that the process started. Nonetheless, I jumped off the table and said "I got this. I can handle this" and tried to do in the natural what was meant to be done in the spiritual. This caused more damage, and by me closing my exposed heart with botched stitching such as wrong relationships and masks to protect my heart, I inadvertently shut out God. This put me in a vulnerable state of mind, body, and soul.

I consider myself to be among a unique group of people in this world. Surviving a nervous breakdown and trip to the mental hospital is not an easy feat. However, when I was falling, God put his amazing hands under me and broke my fall. I could have died that fateful night, but where there was fear, he gave me power. Where there was rejection and betrayal, he gave me love. When my mind was breaking down, he made it sound.

> *For God did not give us a spirit of fear; but of power and of love and of a sound mind.* (2 Timothy 1:7)

May I pray with you?

Heavenly Father,

> *We thank you for your goodness, mercy, love, grace, and provision. Please forgive us for our sin of not trusting you with our brokenness, betrayal, and rejection. We give our hearts to you so that you can heal and give us the mind of your Son, Jesus Christ, so that our core will reflect the fruit of the spirit. Where there is hate, teach us to love. Where there is sadness, give us joy. Where there is anxiety, give us peace. Where there is rudeness, give us kindness. Where there is meanness, give us goodness. Where there is betrayal, give us faithfulness. Where there*

is harshness, give us gentleness. And where we are abusive, give us self-control. We look only to you for healing and strength.

In your Son, Jesus's, name,
Amen.

My Pain, His Purpose

I used to be a strong-willed woman, proud to be me,
filled with my own ambition and ability.
I had decided on a purpose and mapped out my plan.
I put all my trust and favor in the hands of man.
I received some accolades and accomplished a few things,
received a few trophies and a couple of class rings.
I put on my boots and held my head high,
feeling assured with hands folded looking to the sky.
Then arrows and daggers penetrated my skin,
and spiritually I realized my faith was very thin.
I thought I had conquered mountains through
my own strength and power,
unaware of God's protection from the evil devourer.
I called on my mother's God for the peace I saw her get,
but I soon realized with him I needed my own relationship.
My flesh was being stripped, and I felt abandoned and lost,
not understanding that the peace my mother had comes with a cost.
I soon surrendered to God my power, heart, and pain.
It wasn't until then that I traded for peace, purpose, and gain.

Loretta Young, 2019

CHAPTER 6

When Love Goes to Paradise

So while my mother was fighting cancer, I was going through a terrible divorce and custody battle that lasted over a year. My mother, who had been diagnosed in May 2003, went to paradise the following year in February. During her sickness between blood transfusions, fainting spells, and hospital stays, we prayed together, sang together, and talked about my children, my abuse, and my life. I watched my mom slowly slip away from a disease that lurked at her side every moment she took a breath. I saw the light in her eyes begin to dim as she watched us move around her with gentleness and soft whispers. I sat with her during blood transfusions laughing and joking about meaningless things. I lay in the hospital bed with her and told her about her grandsons' adventures. I would leave work and go to the hospital to sit with her and listen to gospel artist Shirley Caesar sing "Jesus, I'll Never Forget." And when hospice sent her home, I couldn't wait to get off work and bathe her while singing "It Is No Secret What God Can Do." My mother loved to hear me sing that song.

Those moments are the most precious to me now. The same mother who wrote in my senior class memories book "Don't blame me. I tried" was leaving me too soon. I could never blame her for what a babysitter did to me or for all my misguided decisions. She was my queen, and I adored her.

I asked her to forgive me for not listening enough or loving enough. My only purpose with her in those moments was to be strong for her, my dad, my brother, and my sons. Focusing on her needs diverted me from the pain that came with the death of my marriage. But let me be clear when I say avoidance doesn't make the pain of a situation go away. It just delays it. The doctors sent my mother home two days before her sixty-eighth birthday, January 31, with less than a week to live. Somehow we organized a birthday party for her and were able to get all her brothers, sisters, nieces, nephews, and dear friends to come to my parents' home.

She requested that hospice set up her bed in the living room where she could see everyone. My mom did not want to be stuck in an isolated back room. She was way too outgoing for that. She wanted to talk to all the family and hear the laughter and see everyone's faces as they came and went. It was my mom's request to see each family member in person so she could talk to them and tell them face-to-face that she loved them.

The birthday party was beautiful! We had cake, balloons, and her favorite foods even though she couldn't eat and could speak only in a whisper. We celebrated her life knowing deep inside that any moment could be her last.

The night my mother went to paradise was still a shock. I had gotten off work early to go by and see her. There was a house full of family, and the atmosphere felt very much like a family reunion. I took my sons with me even though my eldest had a game that evening because I wanted them to see her as much as they could. When she spoke to the boys, I watched her touch each of their faces and tell them that she loved them. I didn't hear everything she said because I was socializing with my cousin and talking to my dad, but I could tell it was an intimate moment for them.

When it was time to take my sons to the game, I went to her and asked if she wanted me to stay with her. My eldest son's game was a big game; his team was in the final playoffs to go to the state championship trials. All my close family members were going to the game that night.

My mom softly said, "No, you go to the game, baby." Then she said words I will never forget, words that I will cherish forever: "Baby girl, I love you, and I am proud of you. Take care of my grandbabies and your dad."

I kissed her three times and held her frail body in my arms, anticipating seeing her the next morning. We all headed to the game as planned, but when it was nearly halftime, something odd took place. One by one different family members would leave the gym. It didn't occur to me that there might be something wrong. The restrooms and snack bar were outside the gymnasium.

After the game in which my son's team won, my eldest son's aunt asked me the oddest question. She asked if I wanted my son's dad to talk to him. I thought, *Okay*.

It wasn't until I walked out of the gym and headed toward my car that my cousin told me my mother had passed away during the game. In that moment I couldn't process what she was saying. It was like some out-of-the body experience.

Imagine watching a championship game where your child is having an amazing game and the team wins to advance to state finals. The energy of all the people around you is so strong, with so much excitement and exhilaration you are overwhelmed with joy. And right in the middle of that moment my cousin was given the most daunting task of telling me my mother had passed away.

I couldn't process the information fast enough, and for some reason I just wanted to be alone. My brother was frantically telling me that I had to go to my parents' home immediately. I was confused and lost.

On the drive to my parents' home, I thought of songs we would no longer sing together—no more laughter, small talk, or sweet kisses. Apparently, the coroner was waiting for us to get to the house to say our last goodbyes. That seemed strange to me, and honestly, I don't remember even seeing her in that moment as the coroner removed her body from their home. I stood numbly while they placed Mom in the vehicle.

My father, brother, and I stood outside and watched silently as they closed the back of the hearse and drove away. They drove away with my mother's soft kisses, her songs, her creativity that enabled her to make beautiful quilts, and the best apple turnovers you've ever eaten. They drove away with my love.

I can't express how anyone else feels when seeing a parent who has passed, but for me it was the most heart-wrenching pain I had ever felt, and I couldn't cry. It was as if my mind was thinking too hard for my emotions to feel what was happening. I remember my cousin coming to my home the following day to pick me up and take me to the funeral home for a final viewing. My aunts wanted me to approve the dress they picked for her, and my cousin was going to style her hair. They walked me into the room, and I saw her on the steel table with a sheet over her upper body, with her head and face exposed. There was a white block holding her head up, and she looked as if she was sleeping peacefully. My cousin cut locks of her hair for my mom's sisters and me and tied them with pink ribbon. I took the hair, not really understanding this strange ritual that would later comfort my soul.

What do you do or how should you feel about losing the one person who carried, loved, nurtured, and wanted you like no one else could and, in my case, would? She was irreplaceable. No person, place, or thing could fill the void. It stays empty, and you are lost. When I was young, one of the mothers at our church told me to cherish my parents and remember that when you lose a good mother, you lose love and when you lose a good father, you lose strength.

When I lost my mother, I lost an amazing love. And when your mother is a child of God, you lose a supernatural love. It's a spiritual soul tie that tugs at your heartstrings. During the funeral I still was unable to cry, and I even read a poem with my brother by my side. When they lowered my mother into the ground, all my hope and faith in God lowered with her. I had believed and trusted her prayers and her God. In that moment I realized that I didn't have a relationship with God myself. Yes, I believed that Jesus was the Son of God and died for my sins and that I needed to go through Jesus to get to God. I knew the Lord's Prayer and the Ten Commandments, and I understood and tried my best to live like Christ, but I didn't know God for myself. I knew God through the testimony of my mom.

When it came to church, I was at a crossroads. I was torn. On one hand I didn't want to go to my mother's church, which was our family church, because it reminded me too much of her being gone. I showed up for holidays and events out of family duty, but I felt disconnected. I didn't feel comfortable going to my ex-husband's church because he and his family still attended. So I went to a friend's church where I didn't have to feel anything.

It took until Mother's Day two years later for me to come to grips with my emotions and feelings about my mother's death. I'm not exactly sure what the trigger was. Maybe my numbness wore off, maybe I was tired of pretending, or maybe it was just time to heal. It's all possible. All I know is that the cry that came out of my being was so deep that it took a whole week to get it out. It was as if an earthquake had hit my heart. I isolated myself from everyone for six months. I have had people tell me that if your loved one dies of a terminal illness, it's easier because it's less tragic and sudden. But no one talks about the aftershocks of emptiness, the pang in your heart for one more hug, phone call, or kiss.

It was at this moment that the lock of her hair became my greatest comfort. I could smell her scent and feel the softness of her hair, and for a moment she was with me. And for a mere moment, I was comforted. There are no words for the devastation of losing your mother too soon. I can tell you that it is one of the loneliest feelings I've ever had.

Holidays can be the hardest of all, trying to get through Thanksgiving without your mother in the kitchen baking and cooking her famous cornbread dressing and sweet potato pies. Even when you manage to use her recipes and cook the meal, that empty seat at the table makes you lose your appetite. For me, Christmas was the worst. It was my mom's and my favorite holiday. Christmas meant a lot to my mom's side of the family. It was when we had our family reunion. It was not only a fun time to get together, but it was also spiritual. It was a tradition handed down by my grandparents. And my parents' home was the designated house where everyone gathered for games and fellowship. My mom and aunts would bake and cook for days preparing for Christmas day. There would be German chocolate cakes, dozens of sweet potato pies, banana pudding, peach cobbler, and my mom's famous lemon icebox pie made in honor of all the December birthday family members. We would play games, laugh, sing, and pray. Every year since I can remember, my mom's brother and his family would stay with us for the entire Christmas vacation. Imagine a house full of fifteen or more people celebrating the holiday season. It was magical.

And because our family Christmases were rich in generational traditions, recreating that magic was a daunting task, but I made the best of it. When my dad told me that I was the matriarch of the family, I felt a weight seemingly too heavy to bear. But I remembered what my mother said to me about taking care of my dad and my sons. I made the best of it and mixed new traditions with the old, not an easy task but blessed all the same. I would go on because I knew that God loved me and he loved my mother, and if he allowed her to pass on, then his grace would provide what was needed to go on with life guided by his love. It would be presumptuous of me to tell anyone how to grieve the loss of a mother. But I will tell you that there is a place of peace that only God can give to help you come to terms with the death of a loving mother.

We prayed along with my mother desperately for her to be healed. But instead of getting better, she got worse. It took some time for us to come to terms with the fact that sometimes God does not answer our prayers the way we want him to. But he is faithful to take us through the difficult, tragic, and heartbreaking moments in our lives as we trust that he knows what is best for us.

In Luke 4:18–19 Jesus says, "The Spirit of the Lord is on me... He has sent Me to heal the brokenhearted, to proclaim liberty to the captives and recovery of sight to the blind, to set at liberty those who are oppressed; to proclaim the acceptable year of the Lord."

Understanding God's timing is one of our greatest challenges in the Christian walk. It is comforting to know that we have a God who knows every step we take, that he has planned and ordained the seasons and facets of our lives, and that he orchestrates the beautiful seasons and the troubled seasons with his love and comfort. It is such a great comfort to know that we have an expected end designed by

God himself. Nothing that happens to us is a surprise to him. He is the conductor, and we are the orchestra playing a beautiful symphony that fulfills his purpose in our lives. This is made so eloquently clear in in Ecclesiastes 3:1–8 (NIV):

> *There is a time for everything, and a season for every*
> *activity under the heavens:*
> *A time to be born and a time to die,*
> *A time to plant and a time to uproot,*
> *A time to kill and a time to heal,*
> *A time to tear down and a time to build,*
> *A time to weep and a time to laugh,*
> *A time to mourn and time to dance,*
> *A time to scatter stones and a time to gather them,*
> *A time to embrace and a time to refrain from*
> *embracing,*
> *A time to search and a time to give up,*
> *A time to keep and a time to throw away,*
> *A time to tear and a time to mend,*
> *A time to be silent and a time to speak,*
> *A time to love and a time to hate,*
> *A time for war and a time for peace.*

Did it hurt to lose my mother? Absolutely! I think of her just about every day. I use the reference of the life she lived as a template for the type of mother, sister, daughter, and person I would like to be. Someday the Lord will call me home, and I want him to say, "Well done, my good and faithful servant."

May I pray with you?

Heavenly Father,

I come to you in Jesus's name, thanking you for your goodness, mercy, grace, love, and provision. Lord, I ask that you comfort my brother and sister as they endeavor to stand strong in the face of heartbreak and loss of their family member. You know what they need, and I pray you gather them to yourself and hold them close. Show them your amazing love and peace that they may hear your heartbeat for their lives as they walk out this season. You are the healer of the brokenhearted, and we ask for that healing now. We receive your peace, love, and comfort.

In Jesus's name,
Amen.

The Moment

If I could find the exact moment it happened, I would be
able to rationalize and erase the memory, therefore moving
forward without a past to inflict pain on my future,
opening new doors rather than continuing to
stand at the door that has been shut.
Whether it is timed or forever locked, it is imperative
that I move toward the unlocked doors that swing
open freely with my turning of the knob.
I must search for new paths for self-preservation's sake.
It is always a lasting question of faith with a desperation of
hope when waiting for the unveiling of a new future.
Promising, maybe? Because nothing is certain but life and death.
Everything in between is not orchestrated by me.

Loretta Young, 1981

CHAPTER 7

When Love Comes Too Soon

When love came again, I had been single for six years. My eldest son was in college on full athletic scholarships, and my youngest son was on track for graduation from high school and enlisting in the Navy. I was promoted at work and back in school determined to get my degree from the University of the Pacific. I hadn't totally given up on marriage, but I was a bit gun-shy. The last one cost me my retirement and my sanity. After having to pay alimony, I was not eager to try again because the cost seemed too great if I failed. Let's just say it was no longer on my bucket list. I figured that a wedding dress and strand of pearls were not in the cards for someone like me, and honestly, my heart couldn't take another break. I dated one guy, but my brokenness proved that I was not ready for a relationship, and it only further validated my brokenness.

I still had a hole in my heart that I felt I needed filled. And instead of going to God, I looked to man. My cousin introduced me to a friend of a friend. He was different than any guy I had ever dated. He was a former Marine like my dad, and he had a Harley motorcycle. He was a hard worker and a breath of fresh air. I could avoid my past with him because he ran in different circles than I was used to. I thought I had hit the jackpot!

After being verbally and physically torn down by an alcoholic person, it was somehow exciting and refreshing to spend time with a man who seemingly wasn't on drugs or alcohol and had no "baby mama drama." His family did not reject me, and he admired all the things my former husband hated and despised about me.

The first few years of our relationship were exciting. I was intrigued at the idea of an interracial, midlife couple beating the odds at love. I was flattered by him telling me that he considered me unique and exotic. He also displayed great admiration for my successes, talents, and creativity—things my former husband seemed to fear. This man adored the fact that I went to church.

It took him two years to convince me that he loved me. He pushed the marriage envelope constantly and used biblical principles to validate his claim. I allowed him to make me feel that if I didn't marry him, I was cheating him out of a blessing God had for us. He even joined my church, accepting Christ as his Lord and Savior. He attended regularly and became a part of the church staff. He was a dependable member and admired and doted on the pastor and his wife. He was persistent about marrying me, offering to pay for everything from the wedding dress to food—even the bridesmaids' dresses. When he proposed to me, he had already asked my dad. I'm pretty sure my widowed father said yes primarily out of hope that maybe this time my marriage would be happy and I would be taken care of if he passed away as my mom had, not an unusual hope for a loving father. Also, this guy was convincing. He proposed to me with tears in his eyes. His approach was respectable, heartfelt, romantic, and highly commendable.

I caution you to beware of any decision made too soon or any commitment entered under pressure. I thought I was now wiser, smarter, and more cautious when it came to love. But my humanness overrode any red flags. This time no one said no because I didn't ask anybody. This guy had done everything seemingly the right way, so I felt no need to ask for advice. More important, he was moving fast. He was so excited and involved that I didn't hear clearly when his parents cautiously asked questions about my decision to marry him.

By the time anyone else started to ask questions, I had cashed the six-thousand-dollar check he had given me, set the wedding date, purchased the dresses, sent the invitations out, and ordered the food and cake.

It never occurred to me that I was marrying a narcissist. And how many women even know what a narcissist is? According to WebMD, the word *narcissism* comes from the Greek myth about Narcissus, a man who "sees his own reflection in a pool of water and falls in love with it." This is only one of the characteristics they display. During my marriage I would encounter many more.

Our love affair started off like someone riding a Harley-Davidson motorcycle one hundred miles per hour toward some railroad tracks with a speeding train in clear view. I saw the lights flashing and the crossing arms coming down. I heard the train's loud warning whistle. And yet adorned in a beautiful satin dress surrounded by sunflower décor, I stood in front of family, dear friends, and coworkers and said, "I do." It was a sad day for a lot of people, but I ignored them. I was still running from myself, my past, my pain, and my emptiness. My pride craved this to happen so I could fill the hole inside my heart. This time I had convinced myself that I had found the cure for my brokenness. I was determined to get my "happily ever after."

I had done all the right things, except ask God. After the honeymoon my husband seemed relieved to show himself the narcissist he truly was. All his time, money, and investment had exhausted the façade he had presented to my family, friends, and me. When my husband finally revealed himself, he acted as if he had won a prize in a huge game. After the honeymoon phase, his narcissistic attitude became evident. I was not his prize but rather his prey, a conquest to be used for and at his will only. Webster's Dictionary describes a narcissist as "a person with an exaggerated sense of self-importance, has a persistent need for admiration, has a lack of empathy for others, has an excessive pride in achievements with snobbish disdainful or patronizing attitude."

There are other experiences within a narcissistic relationship that can take a person through an unfathomable roller-coaster ride. I had been warned to watch out for men who were predators looking to prey on insecure, single, lonely women with good, kind hearts. I never thought I would fall prey to such a person. I must admit I was impressed by my future husband's Latino machismo, Marine Corp values, longshoreman career, and Harley-Davidson motorcycle.

But no matter how many things I liked about him, none of them could overshadow his narcissism. My husband was the epitome of a predator: smart, handsome, romantic, eager to marry, and calculating. He kept his job and resources long enough to marry me and convince me that he was my soulmate and that fate had led us to one another.

I ignored his family's warnings, such as "Whatever you do, don't make him mad, mija," or jokes, like "You don't seem desperate. You're not pregnant, so why would you marry him?" I was determined to prove any naysayers wrong. Together we were going to prove our marriage was strong enough to overcome all obstacles. After all, we were soulmates. I felt so honored when my husband would tell friends and family that all he needed to be fulfilled and happy in life was me. I was so flattered that I couldn't fathom the prison cell I was willingly walking into.

He expected me to save him from his pain, and I willingly took on the task. He enjoyed my effort to try to be everything he ever wanted. Listen. I don't care how committed, in love, and "Christian" you are or how many Girl Scouts badges you have. It is not possible to save someone from themselves. He said he wanted me to save him from his past mistakes, to help him become a better man. I didn't realize until it was too late that he was a narcissistic, chauvinistic, abusive bigot. I know that sounds harsh, but over a course of eight years, I would experience firsthand the effects of each one of these characteristics of my husband.

During the honeymoon stage of the narcissistic relationship, you are on cloud nine. Everything between you seems to click. Yes, there are misunderstandings. But somehow you work them out amicably, and you are amazed at how in sync you two are with each other. I will never regret the beauty of our wedding; it was literally everything I had ever dreamed of except there were no pearls. My future husband made sure it was my dream come true. From the flowers, cake, wedding dress, food, and colors, he was completely engaged. I told him what I wanted. He reviewed it and handed me a check saying, "I want your dreams to come true." He was so excited about the intricate details of the wedding, like cake design, colors, and music. And oddly, he gave me pictures of wedding dresses he liked for me to choose from. I didn't think it unusual for a man to be involved in the wedding planning, but it did strike me as unusual just how involved he wanted to be. However, I thought it was endearing that he cared so much about investing more than just money into our special day.

I will never forget the magical moment of walking down the aisle to Shania Twain's song "From This Moment." I believed the words she was singing, and I believed he did too. At least he said he did. After all, he picked the song list for the wedding. I still think of this magical moment fondly because those memories were moments my dreams were made of. And yet even though the wedding and honeymoon were beautiful, this marriage would become my worst nightmare.

Stop Crying!

For two years I endured what I call the programming stage of narcissistic abuse. For a system to work, the program must be consistent. You must set up boundaries, limits on how far the system can go without shutting the system down completely. For about two years, I went through the first stage of abuse in a very stable way. I had already been conditioned to verbal abuse, and although I hated it, there was a part of me that was numb to it because I was not healed.

It began with seemingly unprovoked outburst of yelling and erratic temper tantrums over simple things, like moving a cup or touching the remote to the television. There were constant complaints of unmet expectations and a host of colorful derogatory name-callings. And even though it was never done in public, it was always insinuated that an eruption could occur if provoked. This instilled in me constant fear that he would lose control at any moment. There were times that he would rant for hours. And then like clockwork, he would become calm, apologize, and then isolate himself.

The pattern was consistent Monday through Friday before and after work. It became my normal. I continuously tried to not upset him by being quieter, nicer, sexier, more submissive, or whatever he considered "better." I didn't realize that I could never be enough because he would always find fault with me, never himself. For the most part, in public he made sure to be the perfect, loving, gentle husband. He was also the most amicable guy at parties or gatherings. He was always willing to help friends, family, and fellow church members. Nonetheless, at home he was calculating, and I came to expect it. This did not hurt me like it had in my prior relationships because when threatened I had learned to shut down my heart and emotions a long time ago. I was not going to let myself feel any emotional pain that would cause me to end up in the mental hospital again. I masked my feelings with the pretense that I was strong enough to get through this phase, and besides, it wasn't like he was physically abusing me. It was just words that he would apologize for because "I had provoked him." I tried my best not to cry for any reason because he made it clear that he delighted in my tears.

When I was younger, there was a saying that "sticks and stones may break my bones, but names will never hurt me." Well, I can tell you that words can hurt deeply. Proverbs 18:21 says, "Death and life are in the power of the tongue, and those who love it will eat its fruit." James 3:7–9 says, "For every kind of beast and bird, of reptile and creature of the sea, is tamed and has been tamed by mankind. But no man can tame the tongue. It is an unruly evil, full of deadly poison. With it we bless our Lord and Father, and with it we curse men, who have been made in the similitude of God."

In the end he accomplished his goals of me honoring his requests about specific things he wanted done. I complied to have as much peace as my compliance would allow.

Hide-and-Seek

His emotional abuse was the strangest calculated tactic I have ever dealt with. My husband would hide my jewelry, underwear, shoes, pictures, and whatever he thought would drive me crazy as I tried to figure out where they might be. I would find my shoes in the backyard, jewelry in shoeboxes, and CDs under the mattress. One time I came home a little early only to find him taking all the pictures off the wall and hiding them under the couch. When I dared to ask what he was doing, he stated that he did not like the way I decorated.

He then proceeded to enlist me in decorating the living room the way he liked it. It was at that moment that I realized I was in a relationship with a person who had issues with control. My husband turned the situation around and accused me of being the one with control issues. Honestly, I did have some control issues. I wanted to control our environment and make it a safe place to love and express love. I wanted peace and security, but it seemed to me that my husband needed something totally different. He needed to have everything his way. It was about his peace, his security, and his way of love, which was narcissistic love.

Securing the Perimeter

Controlling where I went and what I did in the house was another strange tactic of his. He implemented this based on the premise that he was "helping me" and he liked things a certain way. For instance, he did all the cooking so he did not want me touching things in the cabinets. The dishes needed to be in a certain order. I wasn't allowed to go into his office for any reason without asking him first. The problem was that he kept the iron and ironing board in his office, which forced me to ask him for permission to use them. I decided to buy another iron, which made him angry. He took it and put it in his office too.

Things got even weirder when he made the decision that since he had taken on the task of washing all the clothing, he wanted the clothes to be folded and put away in the dresser drawers in a specific manner. This meant he put away all my intimate apparel. Everything had to match. No black panties with a cream bra. That would be unacceptable. He monitored my underwear drawer and organized it like it was on display in a Victoria's Secret store. If I moved garments out of place, he would become livid, cursing me out for hours, accusing me of infidelity. So I bought new underwear and hid them from him and washed them when I washed towels and bedclothes. (Those were the items I was allowed to wash.) It was stressful, and I would be terrified he would catch me washing clothes while I thought he was away.

Don't Let the Streetlights Go Out

Once my husband had established the internal controls, he implemented the external controls. I was told that for my safety and his reassurance, he did not want me out after dark. I initially viewed this as loving concern for my welfare until I accidentally broke protocol. My husband became very angry and sulked because I had worried him. I was to call before I came home. I was allowed to stay at work late if I called him on my work phone. When I went to work conferences and stayed in a hotel, I was required for his comfort to give him the room number so he could contact me in the evenings to say goodnight. I was to never miss his call. Never.

Limiting the Inner Circle

Limiting my inner circle was his other goal. As relationships with family and friends became tense, he began eliminating those with whom I was close. I had already lost my mother and developed an insatiable need to be close to my father, brother, and sons. Friends, who were in abundance in the beginning, thinned out as his behaviors became cold and erratic.

My husband would become agitated when people came over to visit. Eventually, to alleviate the tension, I limited the amount of time he and I spent with those I loved. Soon everyone stopped coming over except for special occasions. It was difficult because most celebrations were at our home since I was the unsolicited matriarch of the family. My husband tolerated birthdays and holidays at our home until he could no longer fake it. He stopped wanting to go to his own family events as well. I would attend the events alone, making sure I was home before dark, and during holidays he would retreat to his office.

Self-Pleasure

Around the seventh year of our marriage, my husband started withdrawing, not just from the rest of the world but from me as well. I felt like my prayers were working a little. The tantrums were fewer, and he spent a lot of time locked away in his study, so I didn't feel as much as if I were walking on eggshells. I began working twelve-hour days. I wanted to be gone before he woke up and to get home as late as possible to avoid altercations with him.

One day when I went into my email on my phone, I found messages from call girls addressed to my husband. It wasn't long before I found out about his private porn addiction. When I confronted him about the call girls, he begged my forgiveness, but he insisted that pornography was not a sin against our marriage. I was so tired of fighting that I didn't care anymore. He kept his affair with pornography, and I kept my peace. I cannot tell you how many nights I cried and prayed myself to sleep. I didn't want another divorce. I wanted my marriage to work. I wanted things to get better.

I felt I had no one I could talk to, so I lay before God and became vulnerable to him, opening myself up to him in way I had never done before. I wanted God to hear and see me like no one else was able to do.

I heard the spirit of the Lord say, "I'm going to teach you how to love the unlovable." This was no easy task, but God was with me. And I stayed, loving, enduring, suffering, and forgiving. It was during this period in our marriage that I realized God had a plan for me, so I made up my mind to love my husband despite the struggle. I waited for God to tell me what to do.

I am by no means advising anyone to stay in an abusive situation. If you are being hurt physically or sexually, please talk to someone and separate from the situation until safety is made for you. I am telling you to seek God with all your heart and soul. Sometimes the Lord says "stay" because he has a plan, and sometimes God will say "go" because he has another direction, but you can only find out what he wants by asking him. "Ask, and it will be given to you; seek, and you will find; knock, and it will be opened to you. For everyone who asks receives, and he who seeks finds, and to him who knocks it will be opened" (Matthew 7:7–8). But you must obey God.

May I pray with you?

Heavenly Father,

We come to you with our broken hearts, broken dreams, and broken expectations. We don't know what course to take unless you guide us. We seek your love, mercy, and grace. We ask that you meet us in our darkest hour and that your resolution will be made plain to us. You say in your Word that if our eyes are on you, then you will be attentive to our prayers. We ask for power, love, and a sound mind in this situation. And may we hear clear direction from you as we wait patiently for resolve.

In Jesus's name,
Amen.

CHAPTER 8

Losing Control

Amazingly, during this very controlling marriage, I managed to see one of my dreams come to fruition. The one thing my husband honestly seemed to admire about me was my being what he considered smart enough to go to college. So in spite of all his narcissistic games and abuse, I finally was able to graduate with my degree from the University of the Pacific. I had earned degrees in liberal studies, child development, special education, sociology, religion, humanities, liberal arts, and teaching. I also managed to get promoted in my career.

My husband decided to go back to school and get his degree. Things seemed promising despite the abuse. I wanted him to succeed, but I was more elated that he would be gone on evenings. He seemed to feel better about life while going to school. He learned how to use a computer, and it became his obsession.

Now, I love Marvel Comics. When I was younger, I wanted to be like Misty Knight. Her bionic arm is cybernetic and incredibly powerful. It gives her the ability to punch a target with incredible force and crush objects made of steel in her vice grip. However, the rest of her body is not cybernetically enhanced. She cannot lift objects heavier than her back, shoulders, and legs can physically support. Her arm's advantages as a weapon are limited to kinetic crushing and impact forces. Just like Superman, all superheroes have some form of kryptonite, something that exposes their weakness.

66

My kryptonite was relationships. Intellectually God had blessed me with the ability to achieve and create, but relationally, I would always fail. I had mastered masking my tumultuous failed relationships with intellectual and career achievement. The mask gave me the ability to excel during relational pain, or so I thought. It took one email to turn the trajectory of my husband's controlling narcissistic calculated plans into spontaneous, uncontrollable physical abuse.

It was then that I realized time was up. I really felt like I had done all I could possibly do to love my husband. I was tired and weary in well doing, thinking of the scripture in Galatians 6:9, which says, "And let us not grow weary while doing good, for in due season we shall reap if we do not lose heart." Then out of the blue one morning, I opened my email, and in my inbox was a video and article (*Pitch*, Kansas City, May 8, 2010) that read:

> *Senior should never lay claim to be a father. The 20-year-old beat his one-year old son, Jr., so severely over a three-day period, just because the child cried, that the boy ended up dying. Senior told police that he pushed the boy down while trying to teach him to walk and later shook him on May 4. He admitted slapping his son on the back of his head on May 5. Later that afternoon, the boy was crying, and Senior admitted shaking the child for a minute and hitting him in the face twice. The child calmed down after being given a bottle. Around 10:00 p.m., the child woke up crying. Senior said he squeezed the child above the waist and poked him in his stomach to check him. Then he threw the child on the floor. The child was unresponsive. Senior then left him for a little while. Senior also admitted to shaking the child two more times, punching him in the stomach three times, flicking the child's genitals and punching him in the groin to wake him up. Senior finally called 911 around 2:23 a.m. and tried to give the child CPR. At the*

hospital, the child was irresponsive, and a medical report showed that the child had a subdural hematoma. The boy's brain was swelling so much that it was pushing down on his brain stem. He had ten rib fractures and multi-layered retinal hemorrhaging. Doctors classified the injuries as "non-accidental" and placed the boy in the intensive care unit. The boy was later declared brain-dead and he died from his injuries. Senior has been charged with second degree murder, child abuse and endangering the welfare of a child.

This shocking article was about my husband's youngest son and grandchild. I couldn't believe what I was reading. I mean, this is the type of horror you see on television. On top of that horrific revelation, there was a news video with family members accusing my husband of being an abusive person, saying that his son learned the behavior from him. It was a nightmare. I was saddened and numb. I couldn't understand why or how something this disturbing could happen.

It was difficult to rationalize that my stepson who had stayed with us for a week several years prior to this incident—a calm seventeen-year-old kid who was quiet, had a peaceful countenance, and was excited about going into the Peace Corps—could do this. *How could that same teenage boy do this horrific thing?*

I didn't know if my husband knew about the incident already or not. I was also concerned about the motives of the person who sent me the information. When I showed my husband the article, it was the strangest moment. He displayed no emotion, no tears, no response of any kind. I was baffled because I had seen him cry when Whitney Houston died, but he showed no emotion for this terrible act done by his son. Instead, he went into his study and didn't come out all night, and from that point on I watched him turn inside himself to a dark place that caused him to be reclusive and even more abusive.

He started slapping me in the face with clothing or throwing things at me when he was frustrated. It gradually progressed from slapping to choking, suffocating, kicking, and ultimately headbutting me in the face. It became so terrible that I started calling the police. You might not understand this, but I didn't want to hurt my husband, and I didn't want him to go to prison. I believed his heartfelt pleas for forgiveness and his promises that he would "never get that angry again."

My husband would go to church and ask for prayer. He would ask me to pray with him at home, and I would in desperation hope our prayers worked. I didn't believe that he intentionally wanted to hurt me. After all, he married me, and I was his soulmate. Nonetheless, I was still being hurt by him. So if my husband didn't want to hurt me, then who did?

I had to face the fact that I kept making choices that hurt me. I was finally tired and desperately wanted to find out why. I didn't know whom to ask or talk to. Our relationship was unique. And we had masked our lifestyle from friends, family, and coworkers. My mom was deceased, my dad was in the beginning stages of dementia, and I had isolated myself from most of my friends and family. I had too much pride and felt there was too much to lose to become vulnerable about my situation. So I threw myself into church by praying, fasting, reading my Bible, and listening to what I call the "three spiritual Js"—Joyce Meyer, T. D. Jakes, and Joel Osteen—desperately wanting to hear a solution to my situation. I began journaling my thoughts and every sermon or Bible study that would give me even a tiny piece of hope or direction.

One speaker said, "God hates divorce." He read a passage in the Bible found in Malachi 2:16: "For the Lord God of Israel says that he hates divorce, for it covers one's garment with violence," says the Lord of hosts. "Therefore take heed to your spirit, that you do not deal treacherously." Then in Matthew 19:9, Jesus said, "And I say to you, whoever divorces his wife, except for sexual immorality, and marries another, commits adultery; and whoever marries her who is divorced commits adultery." So I stayed and allowed my husband to verbally, emotionally, and physically abuse me because I felt that biblically, none of these acts were grounds for divorce.

Now, there actually may have been grounds for separation, but I was not strong enough to leave and start over again. And after all, my husband wanted the marriage more than anything. I didn't believe that he wanted to start over either. I decided to tell him that I wanted to separate from him until he got some counseling. He suggested counseling from our pastor and his wife, which, surprisingly, he was very comfortable with.

Unfortunately, we didn't even make it through the first session successfully. I sat quietly, trying not to disrespect him in any way as he told our counselors how he cooked for me, supported me through college, and loved me more than he loved himself. These things were all very true. I waited to hear him say we needed counseling and a working strategy coupled with prayer because our marriage was failing. I wanted him to tell them how he cursed me often when he was stressed or how he would hide my things from me and how he would lose control and physically hurt me. But he didn't.

I never had the opportunity to speak. We listened to him for over an hour discuss his devotion, love, and admiration for me. Then the pastor said, "That sounds great! Then why are you both here?"

My husband responded, "Because she is ungrateful and selfish and makes me feel unloved."

I interjected by saying that wasn't true, although I didn't mention the abuse. Before my pastor could speak another word, out of nowhere my husband became angry. He refused prayer and accused our pastor and his wife of taking my side. They reassured him that wasn't the case but requested to hear my side of the story. I wanted to talk about the totality of the abuse, but I couldn't, so I discussed his verbal abuse. My husband stormed out of the room and went to the car. Our counselors declared that it would be difficult to counsel a narcissist, so I accepted my defeat. I kept praying, loving, and submitting as I watched my husband become the worst version of himself. And truth be told, so had I.

Within a year of his son being convicted of murdering his grandson, my husband's nephew was killed in a car accident, and his brother died suddenly. It felt like every time we turned around, something bad happened. I had prayed very hard for my husband to change and receive salvation but to no avail. I hoped these tragedies would draw him closer to God. Instead, he became distant and cantankerous. He became depressed and dropped out of his classes, lost his job, and became a recluse. He obsessively stayed in his office with the computer in the evenings. I continued to pray and stay despite him being in another world. I knew my husband was hurting, and I tried my best to be a Christian wife and support him.

CHAPTER 9

Quicksand

Blood, Sweat, and Fears

This may be difficult for most to understand, but I tried to save my husband because I loved him. Nonetheless, the person my husband wanted me to save him from was himself. The problem with his plan was that I wanted to survive and he didn't care much about surviving. It seemed he was willing to take me down with him. He began telling me how he always felt unloved by his father and received little affection from his mother, how the last time his mother hugged him was when he was five years old. He told me how women had betrayed him in his past. So I prayed for strength to be there for him like no other person had been.

Sometimes our love puts us in a precarious situation. It was as if he were sinking in quicksand, and the more I tried to pull him out, the harder he tried to pull me in with him. There is a saying that "all good things must come to an end," and we were close to the end when I endured a night of abuse that would force me to take action to stop my husband's narcissistic pleasure at my expense.

I was going to visit my father and needed to iron a garment. I could have worn something else that didn't need ironing, but I chose to wear a blouse that was wrinkled. My husband was asleep, and as luck would have it, his study was unlocked. I didn't want to wake him because I knew he would drill me about where I was going and when I would return. So I quietly opened the door and took the iron from the shelf. Unfortunately I had to move a sleeping bag to get to the iron and ironing board. Gratefully, my husband did not wake up. I put everything back the way I thought it had been and went to visit my father.

By the time I returned home a little later in the evening than planned, it was dark. I prepared myself for my husband's usual tantrum while reveling in the thoughts of how enjoyable it had been to see my father and brother. Not surprisingly, my husband greeted me at the door. As soon as I put my purse down, he started yelling about me going into his study. I was baffled at how he knew I went into his study. I had been so careful to put things back in the same place. Apparently he noticed the sleeping bag had been disturbed and could smell steam from the iron.

This was insanity at its best for me. I was tired of living like I was in prison. Our discussion turned into an argument, and as the argument escalated, he began throwing things at me. I remember sitting down on the love seat in the living room and saying to myself, "Just shut up, listen to him, and pray."

But my not responding to his ranting made him even angrier, and he knocked over the coffee table in front of me to get my attention. It was in that moment that I became afraid. I knew from the past that in these moments I should stay still and quiet, which might give me a pass on any physical abuse. This time I was wrong. The verbal abuse escalated to physical abuse, and I was terrified. I tried to get free from his grasp when he pinned me to the hall linen closet. He was yelling as he put his hands around my neck and began choking me. I was trying to scream, but my voice kept fading in and out, and it hurt.

Somehow, I was able to get loose from his grip, and I knew that this might not end well. We were now in a heated fight. I surprised myself. I wasn't trying to run. Instead, I was fighting him back. Somehow, I was able to slap him while trying to get out of his grip, and suddenly I felt something in my face crack. I wasn't sure if it was my nose or mouth. What I knew for sure was that he had headbutted me in the face. I felt something warm on my face, and when I looked up at him, I saw blood on his face and in his mouth. I thought if he looked that bad, what on earth did I look like? I didn't know if the blood was his or mine, but there was blood everywhere, and my tooth was loose. Strangely, there was complete silence. We both looked at each other, and I remember saying, "My front tooth is loose." And without a word, he let go of me. He walked away from me, and I walked away from him. I heard the bedroom door close and lock. I lay on the couch thinking about my life and what had just happened.

It finally dawned on me that things were not going to get better. I could not save him, and I desperately needed to save myself, or the next step would be death. Everything seemed to move in slow motion: my movements, his movements, and my thoughts. It was a surreal moment for me and a defining moment in my life.

My thoughts went to a week prior to this incident when I came home from work to a great dinner he had made. I had had a terrible headache and had mentioned it to him. He gave me a Tylenol, or so I thought. The next thing I remember was lying completely naked in the bathtub with water splashing over my body and face and him yelling at me to "Wake up! Please don't die!"

I don't know what actually happened, but he would brag to people about how he saved my life. I couldn't help but think that he might have tried to kill me but realized he didn't want my blood on his hands.

This time, after he headbutted me, I didn't call the police. We were both hurt, and I knew if the police were called, we could both go to jail and lose everything. Instead, I called my pastor and explained what happened. He instructed me to leave my murderous house.

The Great Escape

I waited until my husband fell asleep and then took enough clothes to make it through work, and I left him. I stayed in a hotel for a while, too ashamed to tell anyone what was happening to me again. I went to work and church and told no one. I kept my secret for a week. I was vacillating between going back to my husband and leaving him for good. I decided to drive by the house, and as I drove by I experienced a strong feeling of grief. I knew I couldn't go back.

I finally swallowed my shame and pride and confessed my situation to my pastor and his wife and my god-brother who graciously took me in until I could get my head together. His home was the only address my husband didn't know because my god-brother had recently moved.

When the divorce proceedings started, I did my best to hold it together. I was surrounded by a great support system. But I felt like a two-time loser for getting divorced again for the same thing, abuse. Why hadn't I learned my lesson?

Once again, my husband wanted spousal support and my car, which he had managed to key on both sides after our separation while I was at church. I had to get a restraining order for him to stay away from me. Incredible! The proceedings lasted three months and left me emotionally drained. I walked through the process in fear and disbelief. Most of the time, I was a shell of myself, yet somehow I worked effectively and felt freer than I had in years.

It wasn't until the judge read the summation for spousal support that my reality really set in. I could not believe that the person they were describing was me. It stung when the judge read to the court the following judgment:

> *Loretta presents with the classic symptoms of a battered spouse. She calls the police when threatened or assaulted with every intention of making a report but once law enforcement arrives and the situation is stabilized, retracts her statement. She exhibits the low self-esteem common of battered women, referring to herself as "stupid." This is common when one is called "stupid b***" such as the case here. Feeling guilty about sending the abuser to jail or prison is also a classic sign of battered wives' syndrome. Her descriptions of the abuse are detailed and specific. Her testimony that he pushed her down on the bed and had a peanut butter jelly sandwich*

in his hands and stuffed it in her mouth to quiet her defies fabrication. The testimony is bolstered by the fact that a neighbor heard her screaming and called the sheriff's department. This is not the first time an independent witness had to call the police. It is also noteworthy that during an appearance before the Commissioner in Department 13, the defendant told the commissioner that Loretta was a woman that liked to be hit. The court has concluded that Loretta was a victim of abuse in this relationship. She has escaped the cycle of violence present in the household.

Less than a year later, the Lord blessed me with a beautiful home. I was free from abuse and living in a home with three bedrooms, including an amazing master bedroom, but I was unable to sleep in it because I was paralyzed with fear. Instead, I slept in a twin bed in the smallest room in the house so I could feel safe. I had a desperate need for order and to have everything in its place, and I needed to make sure I could see all my things. I realized quickly that I had not only been verbally and physically abused but emotionally and psychologically abused as well.

I knew I needed help, so I sought out mental and spiritual counseling. I participated in a women's Bible study called Biblical Womanhood, a one-year course study on God's love and healing. This Bible study changed my life. It helped me open up to finding my purpose, and God began my amazing healing process. I also began one-on-one sessions at a women's center.

My graduation from the program changed my outlook on life. It even helped me to look differently at my abusive husband although that did not result in reconciliation. For the first time in my life, I knew God saw me. I will never forget reading John 13 and the Lord placing it in my heart to love the "unlovable," and the Lord helped me do that. Instead of acting like a victim, being the person who was always hurt, I tried to minister to my ex-husband. In fact, when I saw him the next Christmas, I witnessed to him. I told him he was going to be saved and that I loved him. (It's God's love, agape love, as we can never be back together. But the desire of my heart is for him to be saved.) God presented an opportunity for us to get closure, and I was able to ask my ex-husband why he abused me and why he head-butted me the last night we were together.

He asked for my forgiveness and explained that after losing his job and struggling in college, he was angry with life. He said that he was depressed and going through a lot of emotional pain himself, having lost a nephew and grandson (who was murdered by the boy's father, my husband's son). He said he felt I was not supporting him emotionally and that when I went in to get his iron without asking him, I was disrespecting him as a man. He said he wanted me to save him from himself. It wasn't hard for me to have compassion for him, and I was surprised at how much love I felt for him. There was no animosity, resentment, or bitterness. This was not my love; this was God's love.

I told him, "It was like you were in quicksand. I was trying to pull you out, but you were trying to pull me in. There is only one Savior, and that is the Lord, not man."

Through God's amazing grace, I was able to forgive him. I knew that I had truly forgiven him because I felt free. I now know that forgiveness is for my healing first and foremost. It left me with a liberating feeling that made me stronger in my belief in God's amazing power over my life. I came to the realization that divorce and abuse were the fruit of my marriages, the leaves on a rotten tree with roots infested with pride and selfishness.

It was then that I felt the greatest freedom from my past. I realized I wasn't alone, and I wanted to help others feel this freedom. I had asked God for peace and closure. God was faithful to give me those two blessings and much more although they didn't come easily. I struggled with rebuilding my life and allowing God to heal my heart. It is an ongoing process that I am delighted to say is leading me into my purpose. It's ironic that my abuse first came from a woman, and yet my purpose in part is to reach hurting and broken women. What the enemy meant for evil, God is using for his good.

I am excited to go on this journey to my purpose with God. I no longer live in fear, shame, pride, or bondage. I have been redeemed. All things are possible with God; he will never leave me or forsake me. And he will never leave you or forsake you! God's love is everlasting!

The Redeemer

"Fear not; you will no longer live in shame. Don't be afraid; there is no more disgrace for you. You will no longer remember the shame of your youth and the sorrows of your widowhood anymore. For your Creator will be your husband; the Lord of Heaven's armies is his name! He is your Redeemer, the Holy One of Israel, the God of all the earth. For the Lord has called you back from your grief— as though you were a woman abandoned by her husband," says your God. "For a brief moment I abandoned forsaken you, but with great compassion I will take you back. In a burst of anger I turned my face away for a little while. But with everlasting love I will have compassion on you," says the LORD, your Redeemer. (Isaiah 54:4–8 NLT)

CONCLUSION

In my endeavor to write a book about my triumph from pain to purpose, I was concerned about being judged for my experiences. When you are abused, you spend practically every day feeling condemned by verbal, emotional, sexual, and physical abuse. Even after the Lord finally frees us, one of the enemy's strongest weapons is to keep us in bondage.

"There is therefore now no condemnation to those who are in Christ Jesus, who do not walk according to the flesh, but according to the Spirit" (Romans 8:1–2). I want to share with you that God sees you and knows exactly what you are going through. That being said, our faith must be tested in the same way as Jesus's faith was tested. We are strengthened by adversity in our lives.

In Genesis we can look at Joseph's life. His life started out with great favor. But the strength he needed to fulfill his purpose could be acquired only through adversity. Joseph was rejected, hated, and betrayed by his brothers. After throwing him into a pit, they sold him to slave masters and told his father he was dead. He became a slave in Egypt and was promoted by Potiphar to a prominent position but was later falsely accused of rape by Potiphar's wife. He was then convicted, thrown in jail, and forgotten for nearly ten years.

Joseph spent most of his teenage and young adult years in jail in a strange land, separated from his family and everything else he had known. He had no support system. Can you imagine Joseph being convicted of rape in this day and age? He would be registered as a sexual offender registry, monitored, ostracized, and labeled for the rest of his life. But even throughout the difficult times Joseph endured, the scriptures tell us that "the Lord was with him."

When God orchestrates our lives for his purpose, he has your reputation and healing all taken care of. Even when we choose the wrong path, he is still in control. The Lord is faithful to get us to our wonderful expected end, which is the purpose he designed specifically for us. He is faithful to get us there even if we stumble along the way. God makes right the wrongs of his children, his chosen. As we step back and give him control and leave it all in his hands, he is faithful to love us, guide us, and strengthen us.

May I pray with you?

Heavenly Father,

I thank you for your goodness, mercy, love, and provision. I come to you in Jesus's name on behalf of my brothers and sisters and ask that you heal their hearts from what they perceive as a wrong turn, wrong choice, or wrong decision—for we know that all things work together for the good of them who love the Lord. Help them to walk in freedom as you direct them your purpose. Your Word says, "The steps of a good man are ordered by the Lord" (Psalm 37:23). I ask that you begin ordering their steps, and as you lead them, I pray they fulfill their purpose in you and live life more abundantly.

In Jesus's name,
Amen.

ABOUT THE AUTHOR

"The Lord has given me beauty for ashes."

Loretta Everson has been a member of Rock of Hope City and Hope Church. A published poet, speaker, and author, Loretta graduated from the University of the Pacific and studied ministry through INSTE Global Bible College. She holds degrees in religion, sociology, and liberal arts and is an ordained minister. Loretta has a heart for broken women because she was once broken. Loretta works extensively with Inner City Action Dream Center in teaching homeless, broken, and abused women about God's love and salvation. She is an advocate against human trafficking and women incarcerated for defending themselves from abuse. Her passion is helping broken people rebuild their lives through planting seeds of hope in Jesus Christ.

Loretta is the founder of Pearls and Lace and God's Grace ministries. She is a teacher and mentor to women struggling to overcome abusive and violent relationships. Surviving abuse and overcoming the many mental and physical issues that are results from abuse is the driving force that compels her to help other women with similar experiences.

Lightning Source UK Ltd.
Milton Keynes UK
UKHW011310010323
417858UK00001B/5